GOLF

FROM TEE TO GREEN

by

Edwin Stock

and

Jerry Carleton

eddie bowers publishing, inc.
2600 Jackson Street
Dubuque, IA 52001

eddie bowers publishing, inc.
2600 Jackson Street
Dubuque, Iowa 52001

ISBN 0-945483-10-4

Copyright ©   1985, First Edition
                1992, Second Edition
         by *eddie bowers publishing, inc.*

All rights reserved. No part of this publication may be reproduced, stored in a retrieval system, or transmitted, in any form or by any means, electronic, mechanical, photocopy, recording or otherwise, without the prior written permission of *eddie bowers publishing, inc.*

Printed in the United States of America.

9 8 7 6 5 4

TABLE OF CONTENTS

ACKNOWLEDGEMENTS	vii
WHO NEEDS THIS?	xi

CHAPTER 1
THE GREAT GAME OF GOLF........ 1
ORIGIN	1
THE GAME	2
THE CHALLENGE	3

CHAPTER 2
THE EQUIPMENT AND FIELD OF PLAY 5
PLAYING EQUIPMENT	6
THE CLUBS	6
THE PUTTER	7
CHOOSING YOUR CLUBS	8
Characteristics of Golf Clubs	10
Size of Grip	*10*
Swing Weight	*11*
Over-All Weight	*11*
Flexibility of Shaft	*12*
Length	*12*
GOLF BALLS	12
Characteristics of Golf Balls	13
Types of Construction	*13*
Compression	*14*
TEES	14
GOLF BAGS	15
CARTS	15
GOLF ATTIRE	15
SHOES	16
SOCKS	16
GOLF GLOVE	17
HEAD COVERS	17
WET WEATHER GEAR	17
MISCELLANEOUS GADGETS	17
CARE AND MAINTENANCE OF EQUIPMENT AND GEAR	18
CLUBS	18
Irons	18

Woods	18
AFTER PLAYING IN WET CONDITIONS	19
Clubs	19
Shoes	19
Gloves	19
Golf Balls	19

CHAPTER 3
THE SWING IS THE THING 21

DEVELOPING A SOUND, EFFICIENT SWING	22
WARM-UP EXERCISES	26
AND NOW...THE SWING!!!	30
THE ADDRESS POSITION	32
Overlap Grip	33
Interlocking Grip	33
The Natural Grip	33
In Taking a Proper Grip	34
Further Grip Hints and Suggestions	35
THE STANCE	36
Open Stance	36
Closed Stance	37
Further Stance and Address Position Suggestions	37
STEPS IN TAKING THE STANCE	39
Waggle and Forward Press	40
Back Swing	40
Top of the Swing	41
Down Swing	42
IF YOU CAN DO THIS...YOU WILL BE A GOLFER	43
Practice Suggestions for the Impact Area	45
FOLLOW THROUGH	46
FINISH POSITION	46

CHAPTER 4
APPLING THE SWING 49

TO YOUR CLUBS	49
TAKING DIVOTS	50
PRACTICE SUGGESTIONS	51
PROBLEMS AND CORRECTIONS	51
APPLYING THE SWING TO THE SHORT GAME	54
PITCHING	54

CHIPPING	55
Further Pitch and Chip Tips	56
PUTTING	56
To become a good putter...you must	57
FUNDAMENTALS OF PUTTING	58
Grip	58
Stance	58
The Stroke........................	59
Judgment	59
Grain.............................	59
APPLYING THE SWING TO TROUBLE SHOTS	**61**
UNEVEN LIES	61
Uphill Lie	62
Downhill Lie	62
Sidehill Lie	63
HITTING OUT OF HEAVY GRASS (ROUGH)	64
SAND SHOTS.........................	64
Pro Style for Hitting Out of Sand	65
OTHER TECHNIQUES	65
WIND SHOTS	66
With the Wind	66
Into the Wind	67
Crosswind Shots	67
WET CONDITIONS	68
COLD WEATHER	69
HOT WEATHER	69

CHAPTER 5
PLAYING THE GAME............... 71

IN THE CLUBHOUSE	71
PLAYING CONDITIONS	72
SUMMER RULES	72
WINTER RULES	72
PREFERRED LIES OR "PICK-N-CLEAN"	73
HANDICAPS	73
A SCORECARD	74
GROSS SCORE AND NET SCORE	74
MATCH PLAY OR MEDAL PLAY	76
RULES OF GOLF	76
THE TEE	76
FAIRWAY TO THE GREEN.................	78
BASIC RULES - TEE TO GREEN............	79
One Stroke Penalties	79
Lost Ball	*79*
Out of Bounds	*79*

Unplayable Lie	*80*
Ball in a Water Hazard	*80*
Dropping the Ball	80
THE GREEN	81
FREE DROP SITUATIONS	83
MORE TWO STROKE PENALTIES	84
Grounding Club in Hazard	84
Unsportsmanlike Conduct	84
RULES OF SAFETY	85

CHAPTER 6
WHAT YOUR HEAD CAN DO FOR YOUR BODY 89

KNOW THYSELF	89
A POSTIVE ATTITUDE	92
MENTAL REHEARSAL	93
ON THE COURSE - KEEP IT SIMPLE	93
ON ADVICE FROM OTHERS	94
ON TAKING LESSONS	95
LEFT HAND OR RIGHT?	95
ABOVE ALL - ENJOY!	96

CHAPTER 7
KNOW THE LANGUAGE 99

ACKNOWLEDGEMENTS

Rolling Green Golf Club - Huntsburg, OH
Briarwood Golf Club - Broadview Heights, OH
Mirror Lakes Country Club - Lehigh, FL
Riverview Golf Club - Braceville, OH

Illustrator FRED VOLLMAN
Photographer BETH STOCK
Typing HELEN HUDAK

And the thousands of Men and Women...boys and girls...we have shared golf experiences with...who have greatly contributed to this book.

This book was put together with a lot of "T.L.C." because we want you to enjoy the game...as we do!

Edwin J. Stock
Professor, Health and Physical Education,
Cuyahoga Community College-West
Cleveland, OH

Professional Golf Instructor
Rolling Green Golf Club,
Huntsburg, OH

Bobick's Willoughby Golf Center
Willoughby, OH

Jerry A. Carleton
Assistant Professor
Kent State University Trumbull Campus
Warren, OH

Varsity Golf Coach and Golf Instructor, K.S.U.T.C.

With this book, we have tried to reach:

1. The typical beginner...who finds little time to practice.

2. The beginner who becomes devoted to the game.

3. The experienced golfer who is continually trying to improve.

4. The self-made golfer...who tries to learn it on his own.

5. The golf "nut" who may find this material a fresh new approach.

WHO NEEDS THIS?

Having enjoyed and served the honorable old game as competitive players...tournament directors and committee heads...and as teachers who have devoted many years to helping others learn the game...we were compelled by a dual motivation to present this book.

First, it is written in response to the tens of thousands of former pupils we have worked with in college classes, recreation classes, high school and varsity golf squads and in private instruction at several ranges and golf courses. As a nostalgic service to these nice people–with whom we have shared every known emotion during our learning processes–we feel obligated to offer a book which evolved from our common experiences and frustrations.

Secondly, having had enough ability to be varsity athletes (by the luck of the draw), it became obvious that most people had other talents...not necessarily those needed in the golf swing. This observation was enhanced by years of teaching physical education classes and coaching varsity teams on the junior high, high school and college levels. Over the years, we have developed a sincere empathy for the vast majority of people who have difficulty with the golf swing...who find little time to practice and will struggle to play well.

It seems there is a need for a basic instruction book written by those who thoroughly understand the game...and who have worked with people who cover the entire spectrum in a range of ability. *We feel obligated to offer a book which presents a realistic...practical...simple...and yet a light and encouraging approach to golf!*

Let's start thinking right! Any human activity which requires a high degree of skill to achieve even nominal success...requires practice and thinking. To be played well, golf is a difficult and exacting game...one with little margin for error. In our fast-paced society we have many interests and many demands on our time. We are conditioned to expect instant results. Golf does not lend itself to instant success...not even for the most talented. Therefore, lest we become discouraged in our efforts–or are willing to settle for a lessor level of success–we must be realistic in our expectations.

One of the beautiful characteristics of golf is the fact that, regardless the level of skill developed...or the degree of success

achieved...we may all reap the same basic benefits from this grand old game. We can enjoy the challenge...the thrill of a good shot...the comradry and social profits found in the great fraternity of golf...and we can all enjoy the beautiful and invigorating environment in which the game is played. (In fact, the "average" golfer may enjoy the aesthetic values of the game to a greater extent than the better player...who is forever concerned about the swing and every poorly hit ball.)

"Those who feel they are playing badly may find solace in the fact that they are getting more shots per dollar than others...as well as more exercise and a more scenic view of the golf course."

From a vocational point of view, a working knowledge of golf is an important asset in business... a valuable credential to present a prospective employer, client...or friend.

Golf is for everyone! From young to old...male and female...many afflicted with varying degrees of physical impairment–may play golf.

For those of you who become keenly interested in the game...and/or those who already have enjoyed the game for some time...the *discussion* sections will go into greater depth...with more details, helpful hints, ancedotal reflections, practice suggestions and exercises.

Following is a presentation for the swing...the game...the basic rules...the etiquette...and the *challenge* of golf...from people who have played, taught, researched, promoted...and loved this game for many years.

Start swinging...and keep swinging...forever!! Good Luck!!!

E.S. – J.C.

Chapter 1

THE GREAT GAME OF GOLF

ORIGIN

It was inevitable that a game such as golf would evolve someday. Man—and now woman—have been beating little round things with sticks since time began. There is evidence that 3,000 years ago Roman soldiers played a game in which they batted little round "balls" around with curved sticks. Both the Dutch and the Scotch claim the early development of the game. But the consensus is that about 500 years ago a group of Scottish delinquents laid out a course and the game as we know it was born. (Legend has it that...after playing out each "hole"...the boys took a wee nip of Scotch venom...and after 18 holes they were completely blasted. They decided that 18 holes was a nice round...and so the standard of 18 holes as a typical golf course was set for the golf world.)

The rulers of Scotland soon issued edicts against the playing of "golf" because it was becoming too popular and interfered with the practice of archery...which was essential to the defense of the island. But enthusiasm for the game spread and when royalty started to play...the laws were ignored and finally abolished.

The first official rules of golf were drafted in 1754 and many of the original rules still govern play. The Royal and Ancient Golf Club of St. Andrews, Scotland, and the United States Golf Association are the official governing bodies around the world, and dictate rules for play.

Through British influence the game came to America late in the 19th century and caught on immediately. John G. Reid, a Scotsman living in Yonkers, New York, introduced the game in a cow pasture in 1888...formed a small group of players and started us on a national binge. Golf enjoys its greatest popularity here.

Today–about 26 million Americans are punishing better balls with more sophisticated sticks...and have transfigured the old game into...an obsession...a curse...an incurable disease, and, for some, a way of life. Whatever we do with it...or to it...we may as well face it...golf is a great game and is here to stay!

THE GAME

Golf is a beautiful game. It is played on some of the finest real estate in the world. A golf course is a beautiful blending of nature's greatest endowments in trees, grass, water, woods and rolling plains...all masterfully manicured by man's genius...to provide an enchanting setting for a game.

There are no noisy crowds, no whistles screaming, no smelly locker rooms...just nature's delightful and restful sights and sounds...augmented by sights and sounds humans make when content, happy, thrilled and, at times, frustrated and irritated.

THE CHALLENGE

Golf is a very challenging game! It will challenge every function about you! It will challenge your athletic prowess...your thinking ability...your memory...your concentration...your emotions...your self-control, as well as the delicacy of your ego. Golf is exhilarating and humbling...intoxicating...and addictive. It could be such a simple game...and yet, can be a most complex game.

You will learn more about yourself in pursuit of the challenges presented than any doctor will ever discover about you. In one round of golf you may experience every emotion we know!

If there is one single virtue which must be nurtured and present throughout your pursuits in this game...it is *patience!* You must be patient in the *learning process*...accepting valid and experienced instruction, realizing that the human body adapts and tunes into any new revived activity–slowly...and understanding that skill in any human endeavor can only be developed through patient, methodical, systematic practice. If patience is a virtue...in golf it is the name of the game...and tantamount to success! *You must be patient in playing the game*...realizing that we humans characteristically have mood swings...ups and downs...good days and bad. In golf you will have good shots, great shots, and ugly shots! *Impatience* will only interfere with your pleasure and inhibit the development of the many skills needed to play the game. On the course, impatience will thwart the successful application of the skills you have developed through practice and have at your command.

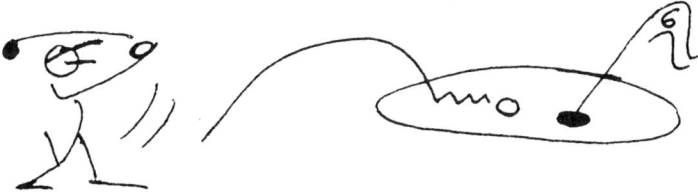

Be patient! Learn, develop skills, and play patiently! Find yourself!!

The objective in the game of golf is simple! It is to hit a hard little white ball with a variety of clubs...with as few swings as possible, from the start (tee) of each "hole" to the finish (a hole on a "green") of each hole.

Chapter 2

THE EQUIPMENT AND FIELD OF PLAY

A GOLF COURSE is 18 different and distinctive "holes" designed by a golf course architect...in and among a given plot of nature's blessings.

A course varies in size from 100 to 175 acres and each hole may vary in length from 100 to 600 yards. Each hole may have its share of trees, hilly terrain, creeks or lakes, and sand traps or bunkers. The starting point of each hole is the tee off area–or "tee"–which is a nicely kept area of grass, from which the initial shot is hit. The desirable route to the hole is the *fairway*, a freshly mowed path of grass 30 to 60 yards wide...wending its way past woods, mounds, bunkers and perhaps a lake or creek, up to the GREEN. The green is a beautifully manicured area in which a hole–exactly 4 1/4 inches is cut. A metal or plastic cup is inserted in the hole which holds a 6-7 foot flagstick, numbering the hole you are playing...and defiantly waving its challenge at you. There are no two holes exactly alike in the entire world. And...believe it or not...you will never in your life have two shots exactly alike. This is one of the reasons Golf is such an interesting and fascinating game!

Each hole has a *par* rating depending on the length of the hole. Par is a standard of excellence and a constant challenge and opponent. Par scores are good scores. A score of one under par is a "Birdie"...and two strokes under par is called an "eagle." A rarity in golf is a hole in one or "ace." One stroke over par is a "bogey"...and two over is a "double bogey," etc.

Par Computations		
Par	Yardages for Men	Yardages for Women
3	up to 250	up to 210
4	251-470	211-400
5	471 and up	401-575
6		over 576

Your score is the number of times you deliberately swing at the ball...whether you hit it or not...from the tee and into the hole. Your score is recorded after each hole on a scorecard...which is available at the starting point on each golf course. Each course has its own style of uniquely designed scorecards.

PLAYING EQUIPMENT

THE CLUBS

These are the tools of the trade. There are two kinds of clubs you will need—woods and irons. The clubs in your set will be of different lengths, with no two clubs of the same length. Each club is designed to give you a prescribed distance when hitting a ball. If you buy a full set of clubs, you will have four woods, nine irons, and a "putter." In a full set, the clubs are engineered so as to give you a 10 yard difference in distance between clubs...ranging from a hit with your shortest club...to a hit with your longest. Most beginners...and occasional players should buy a "basic" set or "starter" set which consists of two woods, four irons and a putter. With this set, you have a 20 yard gap, in distance between clubs.

Unfortunately, someone numbered the clubs in reverse order of length. In a full set the woods are numbered 1-3-4-5, from the longest to the shortest...and the irons 2-3-4-5-6-7-8-9-wedge, from the longest iron (#2) to the shortest (PW). The #2 iron is rarely included in full sets anymore...and the Pitching Wedge is a short distance club which could be called a #10 iron.

Metal "woods" are very popular these days. They seem to be more durabel and more playable.

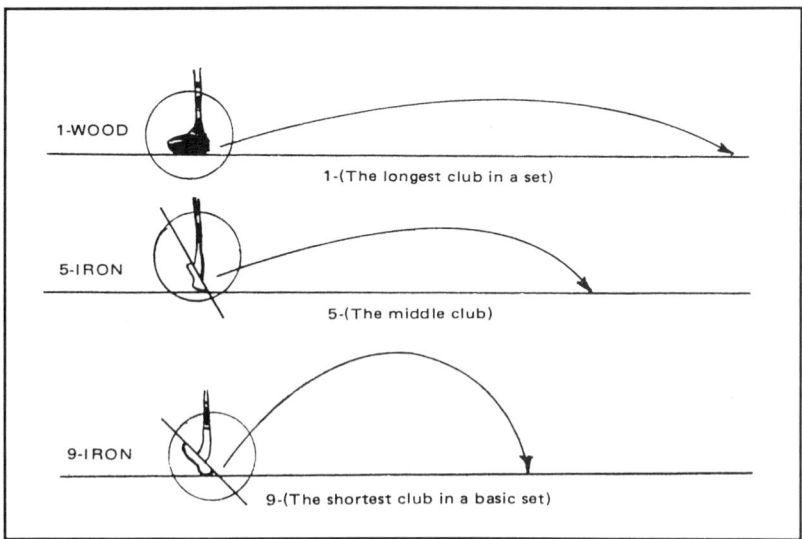

THE PUTTER

The Putter is a special club usually included in basic sets and personally selected to be included in a full set. It is designed to roll the ball into the cup upon reaching the green. It is the most frequently used club in the set.

Each club has a degree of "loft" built in which will give a well-hit ball a prescribed arc...and distance. The shorter the club- the greater the height of the arc...and therefore the shorter the distance it can be hit.

The "range" in your set - from the shortest club to the longest - will be a personal thing...it will depend on your skill, strength and efficiency of your swing.

The graphic below illustrates an "average" range in clubs, if hit well, for men and women. Also illustrated is the degree of loft and the typical arc for flight path for each club.

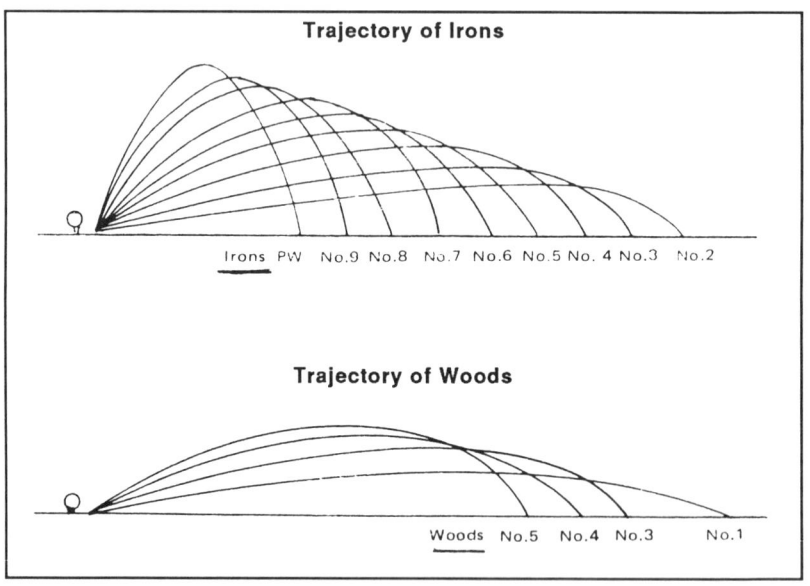

CHOOSING YOUR CLUBS

A set of clubs may range in price from about $80 to $1,200 and more if customized. The basic difference between sets is the amount of "engineering" that goes into them. The cost of materials used is not a significant factor to the manufacturer. In general, the higher the price the more attention paid to balance, "feel" and careful matching of all characteristics in a club in relation to all other clubs in the set.

Beginners and occasional golfers need not buy expensive clubs. They need not be concerned with length, "swingweight", "flexibility", or other characteristics of clubs...not until they become more experienced and decide how seriously they will play the game. 90% of the golfers can play with standard models which most manufacturers make...and are available at pro shops, sporting goods stores, department stores and most discount houses. Women's clubs are shorter, lighter in weight, have thinner grips and more flexible shafts than men's clubs.

Currently, there is a great emphasis on "properly fitted" clubs...suited to your height, swing characteristics, etc. These are sales pitches. You *do not* have a choice in the various factors involved unless you buy expensive clubs. Almost everyone can play with standard clubs.

Discussion

The most expensive clubs in the world cannot hit the ball for you. How often have you heard of touring pros losing their customized personal sets...only to borrow a set for the day...and shoot one of the finest rounds of their careers.

We believe typical golfers would play better if they spent less money on equipment and more on competent instruction ...coupled with meaningful practice.

Golf clubs are a good investment. Unless accidentally damaged by unusual hits...or temper displays...clubs can last a lifetime. Used clubs have good resale value. If you buy a basic set...do not buy with the intent to "fill in" the even clubs at a later date. Simply sell your set when ready to buy a full...or better set.

An important factor to be considered by some people is the "image" they wish to convey. If you belong to a private club...or will entertain clients on a golf course...an expensive, known brand set is probably a must...and serves as a conservation piece.

Discussion

"When you are ready...and able...to buy a set of clubs you will cherish, you should consult your teacher who has seen you swing and hit balls before you buy. If not, you probably should buy them from a local teaching professional who will watch you hit some shots and measure you for a more personal fit."

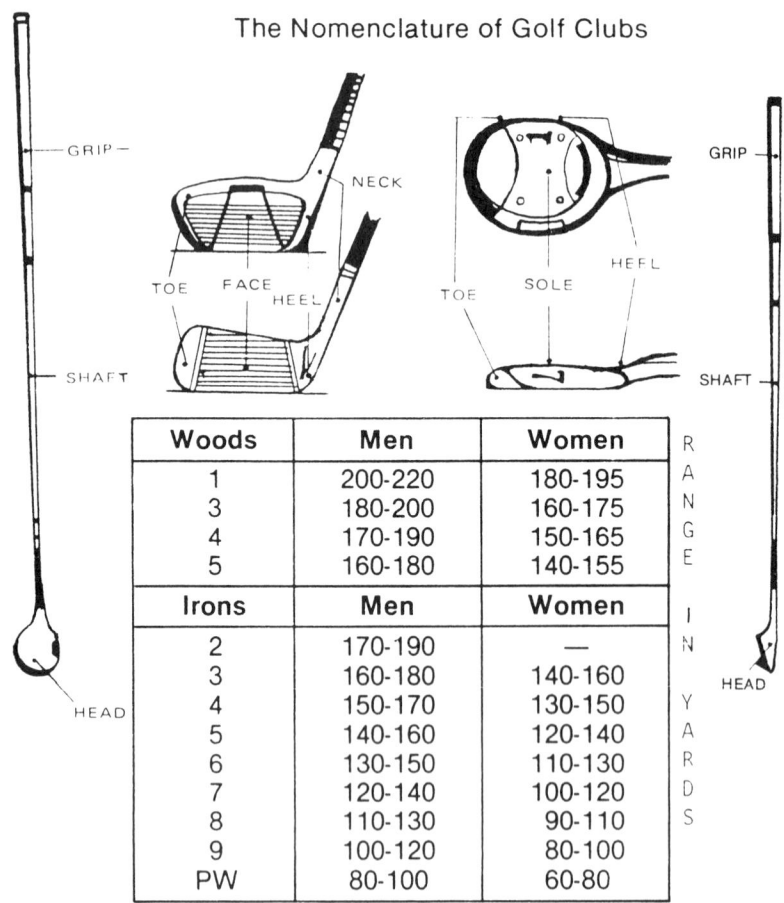

The Nomenclature of Golf Clubs

Woods	Men	Women
1	200-220	180-195
3	180-200	160-175
4	170-190	150-165
5	160-180	140-155
Irons	Men	Women
2	170-190	—
3	160-180	140-160
4	150-170	130-150
5	140-160	120-140
6	130-150	110-130
7	120-140	100-120
8	110-130	90-110
9	100-120	80-100
PW	80-100	60-80

RANGE IN YARDS

Characteristics of Golf Clubs

Following are some of the golf club characteristics to consider.

Size of Grip

Standard for men or women in most sets...but may be ordered 1/32nd or 1/16th of an inch oversize or undersize...if preferred or recommended. The length of your fingers is a factor here.

Swing Weight

This characteristic denotes the proportion of the weight of the club head to the weight of the shaft and grip. In a matched set, as the clubs get shorter, the heads are made heavier to maintain the same "swing weight". Swingweights are referred to by letters A-B-C-D and E. They range in gradation, in each letter category, from 0 to 9.

Most Commonly Used Swingweights

Women	C-3 to C-8
Strong Women Players	C-8 to D-2
Men	D-0 to D-3
Fine Men Players	May range from C-9 to E-1, depending on personal "feel" and preference. The tendency among current touring pros is to lighter clubs...which generate more clubhead speed.

We have seen good results in women playing with men's clubs...and in men swinging heavier clubs. (D-4, D-5). The added weight seems to generate more force and keep the swing in a better path in swinging through the ball. Good players want the proper "feel" to their clubs...they choose clubs very carefully.

Over-All Weight

All reputable manufacturers make the total weight of each club with the swingweight in consideration...so this factor should be of little concern to most players. Lighter clubs generate more clubhead speed...but require a more precise hit for accuracy.

Flexibility of Shaft

The "whip" or shaft flexibility is a factor in club purchase. Most companies make four different shafts:

Light or Flexible (L): Recommended for most women, junior players and senior citizens.

Medium or Regular (M) or (R): For strong women players and most males.

Stiff: For strong, longer hitters. A rule of thumb: If you can hit a driver 240 yards or better...you should consider stiff shafts.

Extra Stiff (X): For some touring professionals and exceptionally strong amateur players.

All standard sets come in medium shafts for men...and light shafts for women.

Length

Here is where the greatest misconceptions are exchanged. The length chosen is generally *not* determined by the height of the individual...but by the distance from the hands to the ground. (Most tall people have proportionately longer arms and may not require extra length clubs.) There are ways to measure this distance: One is to stand upright and hang your arms at your side. If the distance from your extended fingertips is greater than 28" to the ground...you may prefer extra length in your clubs. If the distance is less than 26"...you may choose shorter than standard lengths. Some pros have a measurement in the "set" position they use.

GOLF BALLS

Golf balls come in a variety of prices. The novice or occasional player should use cheaper balls - which have a lower "compression" - but a more durable cover. A novice will lose balls more frequently because of off-line hits. Higher compression balls cost more money. (The best buys are slightly used balls sold...2 or 3 per dollar...found on counters at most courses.) Balls are constructed exactly in diameter (British balls are slightly smaller and are sanctioned for use in America.) The standard ball has exactly 336 "dimples" for an aerodynamic influence when hit which lifts the ball into the air.

Balls are stamped with a name and number (1-8) for easy identification while playing. (No two people in your group should be playing balls with the same name and number.)

Each manufacturer produces balls in a variety of price ranges. Each makes a "top-of-the-line" ball which produces a prescribed initial velocity when hit. This velocity is standardized and carefully tested under supervision of the United States Golf Association.

Discussion

"With today's sophisticated technology, golf balls could be manufactured to travel much greater distances...but there must be a limit. Each manufacturer, of course, will design his balls to approach the upper limits allowed. So don't get carried away by the claims you read...where each manufacturer at times claims to have the "longest" ball. Choose your golf balls for construction, compression, looks...and sound at impact."

Characteristics of Golf Balls

Types of Construction

1. Solid Balls - one piece construction, durable, with low compression, used on practice ranges.
2. Solid Balls with Surlyn cover - good distance and a durable cover...higher compression.
3. Wound Balls with Surlyn Cover - good distance...durable cover...lively center, usually 90 compression.
4. Solid or Wound Balls with Balata Cover (sometimes in combination with Surlyn in the cover) - good distance but cut easily. For use by good players only because they spin more readily which adds to the typical golfer's woes."

Compression

Compression or "squeeze ability" of balls varies with the degree of tightness in the winding...or the flexibility of the solid materials used in the manufacturing process.

Compression Use Suggestions

80 Compression Balls (Red name and numbers)	90 Compression Balls (Black name - Red number)	100 Compression Balls (Black name and number)
Women golfers Juniors Senior citizens Strong women golfers on cool days (under 55°F)	Men golfers Strong women and juniors Strong men golfers on cool days (under 55°F) Women on warm days (over 75°F)	Strong male golfers Men golfers on warm days (over 75°F)

TEES

Golf tees are small pegs - wood or plastic - used to set up the ball and may be used on the first shot of each hole only. (Wood tees are preferred. Plastic ones tend to mark up your clubs more readily.)

Discussion

"Whether a tee snaps in the hit...or where it lands after the hit...is absolutely no indication of the quality of the hit!"

GOLF BAGS

Bags come in a variety of sizes...styles...and prices. If you will play in a riding cart or with a caddy...you may want a large, roomy bag. If you will carry your bag, or play with a pull cart, you should purchase a smaller bag. There are very light, small, comfortable bags available called "Sunday Bags".

Whichever style appeals to you, be sure your bag has these features:

1. A wide, padded, comfortable strap.

2. A pocket for balls, tee, etc.

3. A larger pocket for a jacket or other accessories. Sunday bags usually come with only one pocket.

4. An umbrella socket and strap.

5. Holes in the bottom of the bag for drainage on rainy days.

CARTS

Pull carts may be a good investment for regular players. These fold up for easy storage in auto trunks. Occasional players should rent pull carts. These are available at all courses at a nominal charge.

GOLF ATTIRE

Traditionally, golf attire is very colorful. Golf allows an avenue for expression in a splash of color...for even the most conservative dresser. However, golf is a rather dignified game and dress should be appropriate and in good taste. Clothing should be comfortable...and designed for golf play. Stylish, colorful and comfortable slacks or skirts and matching golf shirts are sold in all clothing departments and at all country clubs and many public course pro shops. (Light colors...which reflect the heat rays should be considered for warm weather play.)

A lightweight windbreaker jacket is a good item and should be carried in the bag in temperate regions. A pull-over sweater for cool days and evening play should be a part of your wardrobe.

SHOES

Golf shoes are special shoes designed with small spikes in the soles and heels...which create a more firm foundation in the swing...and make walking, especially on hilly courses, much easier. Flat-heeled, low-heeled and tennis or running shoes may also be worn. (Shoes with sizable heels are absolutely taboo on a course...as they make impressions and may damage manicured greens.

Discussion

If you play at a country club...golf shoes are a must. They are mandatory at most private clubs. If invited to a private country club to play, you would embarrass your host if you did not wear golf shoes.

In an 18 hole round you will walk 3-5 miles, so be sure your shoes fit well and are comfortable. (Wear them around the yard a few times. Do not do your 3-5 miles in a new pair of shoes!) Your feet will expand during play...so you may want to buy your shoes a half-size larger than street shoes. Prices will range from moderate...to the ridiculous (alligator, snake and pony skinned). The "breathing leather" types are light, soft, easily maintained...and should be considered. All makes come in conservative to very colorful styles. Golf shoes are sold in most shoe stores and golf shops.

Even though golf shoes are manufactured with greater water-proofing characteristics than street shoes...*golf rubbers or rubber shoes* are a good idea in many climate regions. Rubbers are inexpensive and are worn over a comfortable pair of shoes...on rainy days...or early morning rounds when mist and dew may cover the course. (Golf rubbers are also practical for winter hiking and, ugh! - when shoveling your driveway.)

SOCKS

Socks should be absorbent, and of course, sartorially correct. Pull them on with care so as to eliminate all wrinkles and folds. Most women prefer a low-profile, "bootie" sock with a colorful tassel. These also come in men's styles.

GOLF GLOVE

A golf glove is part of the "image"...as well as serving a more practical purpose. Worn on the left hand for right-hand players...and on the right for lefties...a glove creates a better bondage between hand and club handle for less slippage...and offers some protection from tenderness. It is especially important to wear a glove in a practice session because you are hitting and swinging continually. Full-fingered gloves are preferred. Half-fingered gloves tend to curl down with use. Choose a light colored glove for warm weather play. Your hand will perspire less...again, light colors reflect heat while dark colors will absorb them.

HEAD COVERS

Head covers or hood covers will protect your woods from nicks and scratches and should only be removed for a shot. These also come in a variety of styles and colors. You may select a leather or plastic style which are banded together by a leather thong...or a knit variety which come in very colorful styles.

WET WEATHER GEAR

Rain jackets, and complete outfits, are practical if you play a lot, and are a must in wet weather play. These should be comfortable, with underarm vents for "breathing"...and allow freedom for full swinging.

Better bags have a hood attachment which snaps on when needed. The hood offers protection to clubs during wet weather play. These are zippered to offer access to clubs during play.

Golf umbrellas are very colorful...and are carried in a jacket and attached to the bag when not in use. Choose one with a fiberglass shaft. Wood shafts may warp...avoid metal shafts with tips.

Carry a towel attached to the bag. Keep the club faces clean and dry during play.

MISCELLANEOUS GADGETS

There are a myriad of gimmicks and gadgets available everywhere. These may enhance comfort...the "image"...or simply tickle your interest. The most practical gadgets are ball markers, ball mark repair tools, spike wrenches and brushes to keep the grooves in the club faces clean. (Check your spikes regularly; every course has a wrench available. Keep them tight.)

CARE AND MAINTENANCE OF EQUIPMENT AND GEAR

CLUBS

Leather grips may be washed with saddle soap, and treated with castor oil or special products available in golf shops. Rubber - or combination grips can be washed with warm water and detergent, then should be thoroughly dried before putting back in the bag.

Irons

Iron club faces should be cleaned after use by soaking in a pail of warm detergent water and toweled or brushed. The grooves must be kept clean because they are a control factor in hits. Fine steel wool, such as in kitchen pads may be used occasionally in stubborn cleaning. Wipe them with a thin coat of fine oil before storing for any length of time.

Woods

Woods should not be soaked in water. The faces can be cleaned with warm water and a towel... or soft brush...and thoroughly dried. An occasional wiping with furniture polish will protect the finish...and always before storing. If surfaces become stained from tee action, or from paint on a ball, or from use on rubber range mats, these can be removed with lighter fluid or any of the spot removers.

AFTER PLAYING IN WET CONDITIONS

Clubs

After playing in wet conditions, remove the head covers immediately upon arriving home...clean, and let dry. In fact, all clubs should be spread out and thoroughly dry before storing back in the bag. Your umbrella should be opened and allowed to dry.

Do not store clubs in the trunk of your car. Your woods may absorb moisture in the heat and steam build-up.

Most golf courses have people who will do minor repairs and help keep your clubs in good condition...or will refer you to a repair shop.

Shoes

Shoes should be kept dry and clean. Spikes should be kept clean and tight. Your golf course will have replacement spikes...and a wrench for tightening. Most clubhouses have a gadget with two stiff brushes facing up at the entrance. These are for cleaning spikes and bottoms of shoes before entering. Store your shoes with trees in them...or crumpled up newspaper.

Gloves

Gloves should be dried before storing. You may store them in a plastic bag with a few drops of oil to preserve freshness. Gloves are expendable...if you play a lot of golf, you will use several in a season.

Golf Balls

Golf balls need no special attention. Ball washers are located at about every tee on a course. If stored for a long period of time, they should be kept in a cool, dry place. There is some evidence balls may lose compression or "life" in long storage.

Chapter 3

THE SWING IS THE THING

The main objectives in the golf swing are to hit the ball as far...straight...and, with some shots...as accurately as possible. To approach these objectives we need a good swing. The swing is the basis upon which a sound golf game is built. The better the swing - the truer and farther we hit the ball - and therefore, the better we play the game. Proper form...and good play are directly correlated in golf.

> **Discussion**
>
> "Occasionally we may see a fairly good golfer with an unorthodox golf swing. These are people with good athletic ability who are generally self-taught...who may have been champions with proper instruction at the onset".

There is a "classic" golf swing we see among fine players. Contrary to unorthodox styles we may see among good players in other sports, almost all fine golfers look basically alike. Slight differences in form are due to variances in body build...and/or points of emphasis.

DEVELOPING A SOUND, EFFICIENT SWING

Our main goal is to develop a sound efficient swing. A good swing is a smooth, rhythmical generation of power. It is an artistic blending of finely coordinated movements...a blend of timing, balance, power...and skill. It involves the hands, arms, legs, body...and mind. By developing an efficient swing, the smaller person can hit as far, and in many cases, farther than the big person.

Except in the gifted athlete, the correct swing is a difficult maneuver. The kinetics of the correct swing are unnatural...and uncomfortable for most people to execute. Our bodies simply do not easily move in the pattern necessary for a good golf swing. No other physical motion in life is quite like it. (The baseball swing is a considerably more natural movement...and more comfortable.)

> **Discussion**
>
> "We believe that one could take a slice of 100 people from any segment of our population...have them watch the correct swing 100 times...help manipulate and maneuver each person 100 times through the correct form...have them practice the swing 100 times...and we would see 100 different versions of the golf swing".

As you have discovered in other activities, an unnatural physical movement takes much practice before that movement becomes skillful...and somewhat comfortable. After competent instruction has given us guidelines...and a "feel" for the swing, a good swing will require much practice.

Individual Instruction or "lessons" are, of course, the best way to learn the correct swing. However, these are expensive...many of you could not afford them.

Golf classes are an interesting and economical way to learn golf. Most colleges offer golf as a physical education class...or on a less formal basis in non-credit courses. Most recreation departments and local boards of education include golf in their evening adult education classes.

Discussion

"Hopefully, your teacher will be a good teacher...and not just a good player. A good teacher will have had experience working with all types of golfers...at all levels of skill. There are many excellent players who are not good teachers...who may have little empathy or patience for the typical person attempting the golf swing. (A gifted athlete sometimes has difficulty understanding that not all people can learn skillful physical maneuvers with ease.)"

Along with good instruction, we need to see good golf swings in action. *We should watch as many good swings as possible.* Television offers us the finest golf swings in the world...about 20 weekends per year. Films of great swings are available for class use. *We need a clear mental picture of a good swing!* (Unfortunately we will not see many good swings on a golf course on any given day.) These are quite rare. If you have an opportunity to play behind good players...or to watch them on your course...reinforce your mental picture of a good swing...continually.

Try to imitate good players! Specifically, try to watch good swingers who resemble you in body build. (If you are tall and lean, copy the style of a good tall and lean swinger. If you are stocky...your swing pattern will develop much like that of a good stocky player.) Young people are great mimics. They are much easier to teach than adults. Besides being more flexible and less inhibited...they learn more easily by imitation...than by conversation.

Imitate good players

      Golf books and articles written by golf greats are interesting...we are always fascinated by what the best have to say...but they are of limited learning value to the typical golfer. The great players practice 1 - 3 hours per day...every day! They work on the finest rudiments of the swing. If a fault or problem in their game develops, they may spend *hours* on the practice range...usually under expert fellow supervision...working it out. (We tend to work on our whole swing with one bucket of balls.) In most cases, their suggestions and tips are excellent...having been developed through great playing experiences and many hours of practice. You would need to also spend hours in practice for *each* tip before you could incorporate it into your swing or game. (Ask yourself..."How many hours per day am I practicing? Or per week...month?")

      To develop a sound, efficient swing and a satisfying golf game we must:

1. Experience competent and empathetic instruction.

2. Watch visual aid programs which demonstrate good swings.

3. Take every opportunity to observe good swings in action.

Discussion

"If the Pro Golf Tour...men's or women's...stops in your community - or nearby - this could be a fine learning experience. Besides the excitement and pageantry...and displays of great shotmaking...watch the fine swings in action. We would suggest a visit to the practice area where these great players will warm-up each day. Pick out someone who resembles you in body build and watch...watch and learn! Get a clear picture in your mind of a good golf swing."

4. Read selective books and articles...but read objectively...and with a realistic awareness of your limitations. There are several excellent teaching texts written by fine players...past and present. Check out your local library.

5. Practice...practice...practice!

Do not become discouraged in your efforts. A good swing is a challenge...which takes time and patience to develop. Most of us will try to learn with limited practice opportunities...and perhaps limited athletic prowess and ...experience. But, keep in mind, regardless the effort expended or degree of skill developed...we will all reap the enjoyable benefits of the great game of golf! *We will all swing...one way or another Let's face the challenge of a good golf swing!*

WARM-UP EXERCISES

Discussion

"It is a good idea to warm up before any physical activity. The research is overwhelmingly in favor of a regular warm-up routine...prior to activity...for physical and mental reasons. Golf - with its premium on precise, rhythmic, coordinated movements - demands great flexibility. (We know and appreciate the value of warming up for almost all sports activities...and it is routine in most sports. But in golf...a typical weekend player races to the course...jumps out of his car...gulps down a few donuts and coffee, impatiently waits for his turn on the tee...tees up...and hopes to whack the ball far and true down the fairway! This is absolutely ludicrous! He then starts his scenic journey around the course...analyzing his swing with every miss-hit, listening to the traditional stream of advice from fellow players...and, trying to remember what the great golfer told him to do in the magazine he read last night!"

With the small margin for error in producing good shots, a warm-up seems necessary. Before you start each practice session or game - WARM-UP!

Here are several exercises which will loosen and stretch the muscles you will use...enhance flexibility...rehearse and actual body movements used in the swing...and simply make you feel better!

Discussion

"There are many versions of the time, order, type, etc....everyone may have a favorite routine. The nice thing about any sensible exercise routine is that it will work...if practiced regularly... and with spirit."

1. **Overhead Stretch**
   Assume position shown...with hands crossed on club. Reach up...stretch and hold...hold for 12 seconds. Relax...5 seconds. Now once more...reach for the sky! Hold for 12 seconds...and relax.

2. **Hang Stretch**
   Bend over with knees slightly flexed. Hang the club down and hold...don't bounce! Hold for 12 seconds, straighten up and relax for 5. Repeat...hang for 12 and relax for 5.

3. **Twist Stretch**
   Bend over...twist and reach left hand over to right toe. Right arm extended in air. Looking at the ground...hold for a count of 12. Relax for 5...now twist right hand over to left toe...reach over and hold for 12... relax for 5...repeat left...and right.

4. **Lie down on your back**...bring knees to chest...and roll back and forth 6-8 times. (This feels so good!) On you last roll come out with feet spread...lean over...and reach as far as you can with little strain. Try to reach your toes if you can...or settle for your shins. (With practice, you will be amazed at how rapidly you will increase in flexibility. The body responds beautifully to regular exercise.) Head down...stretch and hold...12 seconds. Relax for 5, stretch and hold again, for 12. Relax.

> **Discussion**
>
> "If you will be playing within an hour, these exercises can be done at home prior to leaving for your game...or practice. If you do not feel sheepish, do them at the course. Not everyone warms up...only the good ones! And remember: maybe you now know something the others don't!"

A simple stretching routine such as the previous one is an excellent way for anyone to start each day. It will make you more flexible...and better prepared...for any of the myriad of motions we go through each day. I am convinced...that many older people...who experience aches and pain throughout each day...and attribute them to 'age'...or arthritis...start each day in pain after reaching over and pulling on socks...or bending over to pick-up something immediately upon rising. Any of us will become inflexible if we are sedentary for any length of time. We would recommend a simple stretching and light calisthenics routine each day - before any other physical activity. It would loosen and warm-up muscles and joints...make us more flexible...and much better prepared to face the motions of the day. We would feel so much better and, I would guess, much 'arthritic' pain would disappear."

The second part of a warm-up routine should include a series of light calisthenics.

5. **Bend over**...dangle arms... shake easily and loosely. Loosen up all the way through the fingers.

6. **With club over head**, feet comfortably apart, and knees relaxed, twist back and forth slowly...6 times in each direction.

7. **Same positions** as (6). Bend to each side 6 times in each direction.

8. **Arms firm** and out to the sides. Make large circles in each direction ...and then several small circles in each direction.

These next two exercises are important because, if done correctly, they also rehearse two of the body motions used in the golf swing.

9. **Club in position** as shown and feet about shoulder width apart...knees flexed. Keeping the head steady, twist the butt end of the club down toward the ground using your left side...and at the same time...shifting your weight to the right leg...now twist the head of the club down using your right side and smoothly transferring your weight to the left leg. Back and forth - 6 times each way.

10. **Stand with feet** shoulder width apart, knees flexed, and club in position as shown. Swing club from left up to right while transferring weight to right leg. Now...back through the "hitting area"...and up the left side while smoothly shifting the weight to the left. Back and forth, each time you swing through the hitting area...kick your right knee in. This will be a valuable emphasis in our full golf swings.

Rehearse this at odd moments in the day. Use a yardstick...or broom. If leg and body motion is one of your problems with the swing, this is an excellent exercise for you.

AND NOW...THE SWING!!!

Keep in mind...the ideal way to learn the golf swing is to carefully watch a good swing...and try to mimic it. Try to copy every phase of a good swing...then have an experienced teacher check your version of the swing and make some suggestions. Then rehearse your swings, over and over again. Work on the one or two areas which seem to be difficult...and try to blend a smooth, controlled, rhythmic *swing*.

For teaching purposes, we will break the swing into several phases. We will point out factors in each phase...and the probable problem areas.

Even though we promote the idea of one long, continuous coordination of efficiency and power...it is more practical to think of the swing in segments...or phases.

Each of us will experience "hang-ups"...phases in which we will have difficulty with the swing, while attempting to find a good pattern or style to our swing. We can take each difficult phase and rehearse it...work at it...over and over, until it looks good to our instructor...and until it feels more comfortable...then blending it with the other phases, in one continuous fluid motion.

Discussion

"Proponents of teaching the swing as one continuous motion...in the final analysis...refer to segments of the swing continually. Error analysis charts breakdown the swing into components. Your teacher will point out errors in specific phases of your swing and will work on these with you. The swing is demonstrated in segments, in visual aids and in exhibitions. In essence...we learn, rehearse and correct the swing in phases. We will look at the correct swing as it passes through these phases and see where you may encounter difficulty."

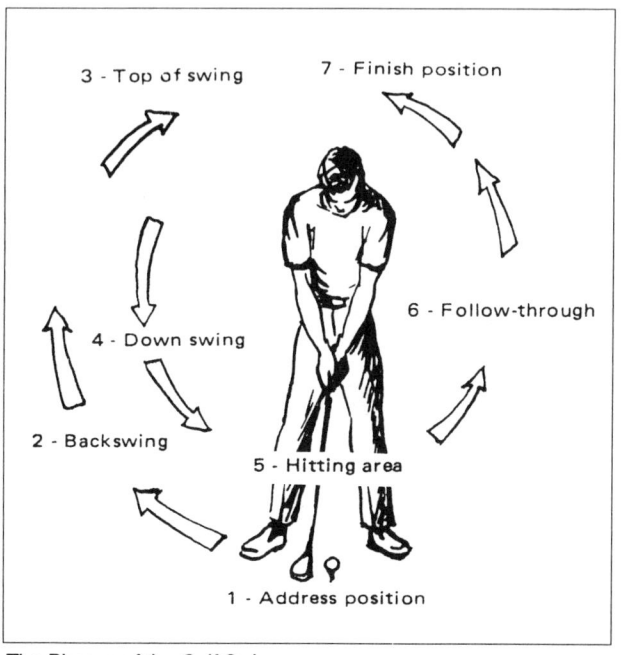

The Phases of the Golf Swing

THE ADDRESS POSITION

A proper grip is essential since all the body and leg action in a swing is transmitted into the ball through the hands.

There are three types of grips. After trying several swings with each, you will choose one which feels most comfortable...and which gives a confident feel on the club. From a top view, all grips will look alike. It is the finger arrangement underneath which differentiates the three types.

Overlap Grip

The Overlap or Vardon Grip is the most popular grip. Most of the fine players use this grip because it enhances coordination between the hands in a swing. It is also the most uncomfortable and most difficult to learn...and it is *not* for everyone. The overlap should be used by most men players, strong and regular women players and junior players with larger hands.

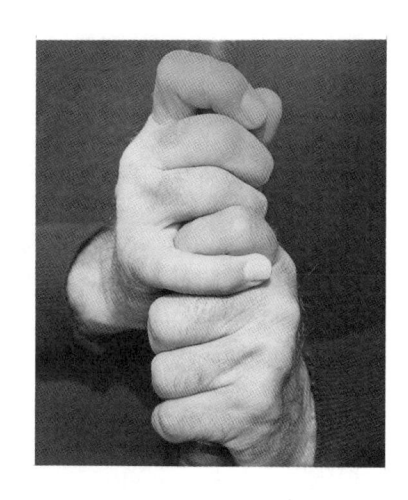

Interlocking Grip

The Interlocking Grip is used by many golfers. The hands are close together and will coordinate well. There is less "feel" with this grip because two fingers are off the club. People with short fingers should try the interlocking grip.

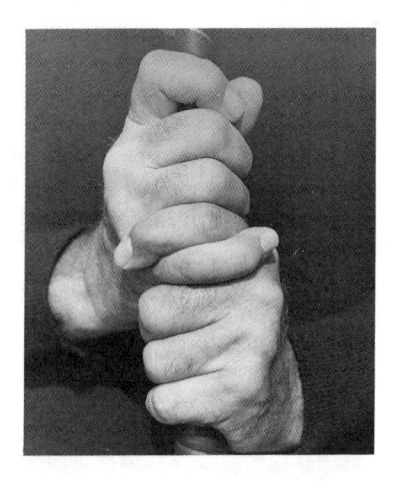

The Natural Grip

The Natural or 10 Fingered or Modified Baseball Grip may feel most comfortable and strongest to beginners and occasional players. It is easy to learn and puts 10 fingers on the club for a maximum feel. It is recommended for people with smaller hands - most women, youngsters, and for men golfers who cannot take the time to get comfortable with either of the other two.

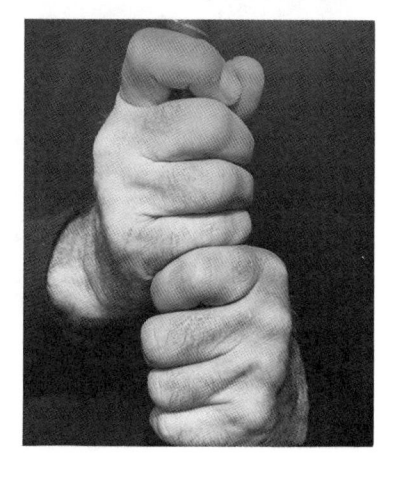

Discussion

"There are fine players using each of the grips. Try them in several swings each...and then choose the one which feels best for you. The one you feel most secure and comfortable with is the one which will work the best for you.

Too often I have seen husbands, fathers, and boyfriends insisting on their captive *students* using the overlap grip - *like the pros do.* I have watched wives, girlfriends and youngsters...with small hands...struggling to capture the grip. In many cases, they will overlap with two fingers of the right hand because they are gripping hard for security - and cannot even feel what they are doing under the grip."

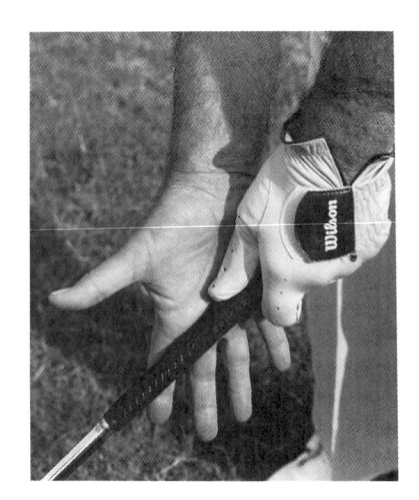

In Taking A Proper Grip

1. Assume a "praying" position with the hands...palms facing each other.

2. Rotate both hands slightly to the right...

3. Grip the club; using one of the three finger arrangements shown on page 33.

Further Grip Hints and Suggestions

1. Women, youngsters...and any golfers not playing well, should grip down about 3/4" lower on the shaft.

2. In the proper "feel", the left hand feels the club in the palm and fingers...while the feel in the right hand is with the fingers only. The greatest pressure is with the last three fingers of the left hand and the middle two of the right.

3. The grip, or pressure on the club should *not* be tight!...no tighter than a casual handshake. Men will tend to grip the handle tightly...which tightens arm and shoulder muscles...which restricts the flexibility needed in a fluid swing. Check your grip at the address. You should be able to lift the club and flex the wrists comfortably.

Discussion

"People who grip too tightly will also tend to pick the club up too rapidly in the backswing. If the club turns in your hand at the hit...it is *not* because you are not gripping firmly enough...it is because the path of your swing is across the ball (not square at impact) which forces the club to sting...or turn."

---

4. The thumb of the left hand should fit snugly in to the "lifeline" crease in the right hand.

5. As you look down on your grip from the address position, you should see one or two knuckles of your left hand. If you see three or four...your hand is rotated too far towards the right.

6. Right palm faces the intended target...or line of flight. Like "shaking hands with a midget"...would give you a good right hand position...then the left palm faces the right.

7. The grip will feel uncomfortable in the learning stage because it is unique. It will become more comfortable with practice. Check your grip constantly...so that you are getting used to a correct grip.

8. Keep uniform pressure on the club throughout the swing. The tendency will be to loosen at the top...and at the finish of the swing.

Discussion

"When playing the game you cannot think about too many details in the swing. On the course factors such as distance, club selection, wind and weather conditions, terrain and lies of the ball are what you will be concerned about. Hopefully, the swing will be skillful enough so that you will simply apply it after considering the factors above.

Realistically...your main problems on the course will concern a faulty swing...so you *will* be thinking about some of the things you worked on in practice. You are *playing* the game...you cannot constantly rehearse your swing - trying to figure out why you are not hitting the ball better. Boil it down to one or two key basics you can use on the course.

An excellent key concerns the grip: Check your grip to see if your hands are placed correctly. If they are, your right palm is facing the same direction as your club head and will do whatever your right hand does...so in each swing and hit, put the right palm out through the ball as you would want the club face to do.

THE STANCE

Feet comfortably apart - about shoulder width, toes pointed slightly out and in the line to your target. This is the "square" or "parallel" stance and can be used for all shots in golf.

There are two other stances which can be used by choice...and in some situations:

Open Stance

The Open Stance (left foot pulled back from target line) is used by most players when using short irons...particularly in short shots around the green. Stocky, heavy-set people may also get through the ball better using the open stance for all shots. Experienced players will open the stance when purposely trying to hit a spinning shot to the right (fade).

SQUARE   OPEN   CLOSED

Closed Stance

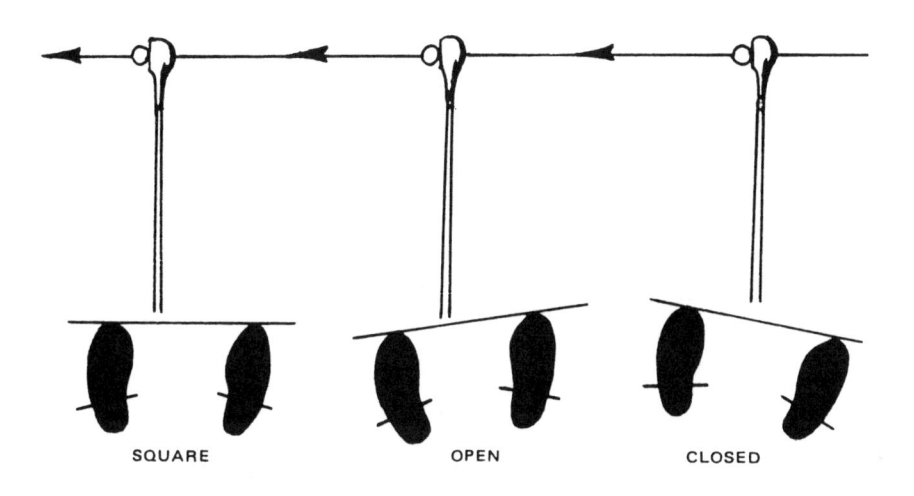

The Closed Stance (right foot pulled back from target line) may be tried by lanky people to get a better swing out through the ball. Also used by experienced players to produce a "draw"...right to left action on the ball.

Discussion

"To keep the game more simple - you may use the square stance for *every* shot in golf. Fine players practice *trick* shots for special situations on the course. They practice them regularly. You will probably have difficulty finding time to practice the basics...*so keep it simple!*

Further Stance and Address Position Suggestions:

1. The weight is evenly distributed between the feet with it centered in the middles to the heels.

2. After some experience, start pointing your right foot straight ahead wile keeping the left toe slightly out. This will enable you to put more "kick" into your swing.

3. In the address position or set-up...picture a *straight line* from the top of the left shoulder slanting down to the club head...just as though your left arm is an extension of your club.

4. Your right arm is more relaxed and tucked into your right side.

5. The hands (on every shot in golf) belong just inside the left knee. This is a very important fundamental...and one which is commonly abused.

6. The straight line referred to in (3) may vary in degree of slant with the position of the ball.

Discussion

"For the typical golfer, three ball positions are suggested.

(1) For all tee shots. Ball is on a line to the left heel.
(2) For grass shots using long clubs (#5 iron and longer). Ball is on a line about 2" inside the left heel.
(3) For grass shots using short irons (#6 and shorter). Ball is played in the middle of the stance.

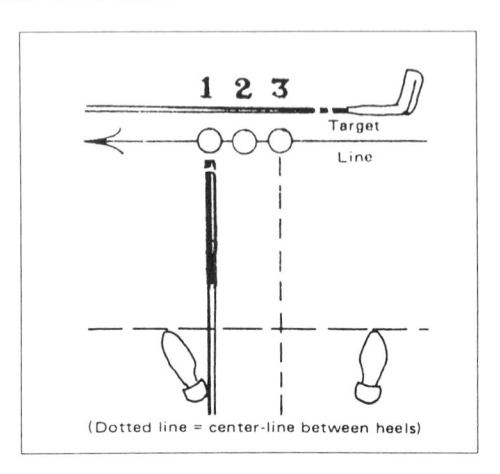

(Dotted line = center-line between heels)

The hands *remain inside* the left knee regardless of where the ball is played.

Except when they want to put a special effect on the ball, most pros play every shot off the left heel...and vary the width of the stance for shorter clubs. The pros all have a great "extension" through the ball...which we do not see in most amateur players. Most of us will have better luck varying the ball position.

7. Keep the knees relaxed. Bend forward slightly at the waist. Butt out...as though you were sitting at the edge of a tall stool.

8. Keep the right elbow a bit relaxed...lower than the left...and tucked into the right side.

9. In the side view, note that there is a break in the straight line from the shoulder to the club head. A plumb line from the eyes would hit you in the hands.

10. The distance you stand from the ball is determined by the club you are using. You will assume the same body position...with the same body set and feel...for all full swing shots. Your distance from the ball is the length of the club as you set it behind the ball.

11. Align the club head carefully. Look at the *bottom* edge (sole) and position it so that it is perpendicular to the target line...or line across your toes.

STEPS IN TAKING THE STANCE

Place your club face center (sweet-spot) squarely up to the ball. Picture a line through the ball to your target. Step back and assume a comfortable stance with your toes parallel to the target line. (With practice you will line yourself up more easily...and correctly.)

Discussion

"Many people have difficulty lining up correctly to the target line. Try pointing your left arm out at the target and then squaring your shoulders, hips, and toes. Many others think they are not lining up properly when in reality their shots are off line due to a swing error. If you are having problems, have someone stand behind you as you hit to check your alignment."

"Waggle" and Forward Press

It is awkward to go from your set directly into your swing. A "waggle" is a preliminary, auxiliary motion which loosens you up and gives you a pre-swing rhythm. With practice, you will have your own personal "waggle".

After a few waggles, there is a momentary pause as you set the club face down behind the ball one last time...then slightly "press" to the left before going into a backswing. The press will be felt in the right knee or in the hands or both.

Note: If the waggle and forward press are awkward or confusing, don't use them until you are more experienced...at which time, they will become a natural prelude to your swing.

Back Swing

1. Take the club back away from the ball in a low, straight path with the entire "line" (from the left shoulder to the club head). As your body turns, the club path will come to the inside.

2. Keep your left arm firm and as straight as you can without straining. (Picture the path of your club head as the circumference of a large wheel. With practice and conditioning, it will be easier to take the club back smoothly...with the firm left arm acting like a "spoke" in the wheel.)

3. As you turn back away from the ball, your left shoulder comes in under the chin. Get a full turn as your shoulders pivot.

4. The right elbow points down as you go into your backswing.

5. The wrists start cocking as you pass the hips...and smoothly flex as you come up to the top of the swing.

6. Your weight has shifted to the *inside* edge of the right foot. The left knee flexed in and the left heel rises *only as much as you need* to for comfort.

7. Keep the backswing smooth and controlled. You are simply "winding-up"...taking the club up into hitting position...from which you will smoothly accelerate back into the ball.

Discussion

"Too many golfers (especially the guys...and particularly on the first tee) have backswings which are *too fast.* We all want to hit the ball a long way, but you don't want to use your power going *away* from the ball. Build it up and save it for the swing *back into* the ball."

Top of the Swing

1. There is a slight pause at the top as you are changing direction.

2. Left arm is still firm but not tight.

3. Club shaft is in a position about parallel to the ground. (Heavy-shouldered people may not reach this high...while limber, flexible golfers...particularly women and juniors...may go beyond the parallel and still have good control.)

4. Check to feel that hands have *not* loosened on the club. (Women in particular will tend to loosen the club in the left hand at the top of the swing.)

5. Right elbow is pointed down and upper arm is parallel to the ground.

6. *Keep the head steady* throughout the backswing!

Down Swing

1. One of the critical points and a major difference between fine swings and all others, is the *start* of the down swing. In a good swing, the *first move* from the top is a *lateral shift* (lateral movement in through the legs and/or left hip) back toward the ball. This sets up the swing for a path through the ball with *both arms extended*, as all good players do. Try not to start with a twist to the left...which makes it impossible to swing out and forces the swing to come in a path *across* the ball...from right to left...which will make the ball do weird things.

Discussion

"From our observations, we would guess 90-95% of all men golfers and about 50% of all female golfers *swing across the ball*. Women are more relaxed and flexible and are able to come through the ball in a straighter path...and will tend to hit straighter shots. Next time you are on the course check out the mixed groups. You will notice the gals are in the fairway, while the guys are off somewhere in the woods.

---

2. As our swing shifts laterally to the left, the weight transfers to the left foot...accentuated by a "kick" in the right knee.

3. The wrists remain cocked as they approach the ball...releasing like a coiled up spring at the last instant...unleashing wound-up power *through* the ball. The typical golfer releases the wrists too soon...many at the start of the swing from the top...losing much power before coming to the ball...and getting a sweeping action, instead of a good smack into the ball.

The Swing is the Thing 43

IF YOU CAN DO THIS...YOU WILL BE A GOLFER

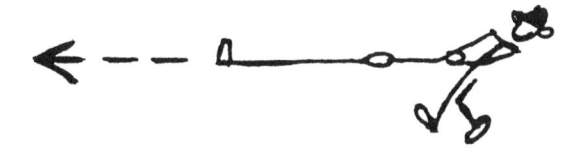

Here we find the one most significant difference between good swings and all others. Here is where we "separate the men from the boys"...why many little guys can out hit many bigger guys...and why there are not more good golfers in the world! This is the most unnatural feel of all and the most difficult position in the swing to learn and to teach. The challenge in the golf swing now becomes most interesting.

1. Keep good balance as the weight smoothly slides to the left side.

2. Right knee is coming in hard.

3. The club head catches up with the hands, but *do not* allow it to pass the hands by "snapping" it through.

4. At impact, your "shoulder-to-club head" line should be firmly passing through the ball.

5. Concentrate on making *good* contact... club face *squarely* through the ball. Try to *see* the club head hit through the ball. (This is *not* possible but it will help keep your head steady.)

6. Keep the head steady...a little behind the ball. A line from your left eye would drop on top of the ball.

7. Keep eyes on the ball.

8. Right elbow brushes by right hip as it remains close to the side...just before both arms extend out through the ball.

9. Both arms are straight and *reaching out* after hitting through.

Fine players make few mistakes in their swings. When they do, they will make them in the impact area. They call it *coming off the ball.*

The extension through the ball is unnatural for *everyone* and will probably never feel comfortable for most of us because we cannot practice enough.

Discussion

"Because this phase of the swing will surely determine whether you will be a *good* golfer, or just another player, let's give you a few more tips. See if any of these will "click" with you as a guideline to use in practice and play.

1. Squeeze your left hand at impact.
2. Pick a spot in front of the ball on the line to the target. Try to swing out over the spot.
3. The back of your left hand should be flaring out to the target.
4. Your club head will do exactly what your right palm will do, so smack the palm into the ball!
5. For you guys who cannot overcome your old baseball swings, the right shoulder should be *lower* than the left at impact.
6. In good swings, the hands *pronate* fast at impact. The right hand is coming up toward the left, which, if timed right, squares the club at impact. This is the prime objective in any swing.
7. *Point* your right thumb at your target as you extend through the hit.

Practice Suggestions for the Impact Area

1. Keep a second ball in front of your target ball as you practice. Try to swing out over the second ball after you hit.

2. Swing out and point your right thumb in this drill.

3. Exercise - Drill.

Point left hand at target.

Do not move the left hand as you swing up with right.

Rehearse this phase of the swing over and over again. Get used to sliding out, with right shoulder down, into the "extended position".

This is a good drill...practice it regularly. Be careful to take only slow, half-swings!

FOLLOW THROUGH

1. Keep head steady and down until your right shoulder comes up under your chin.

2. Hands continue out and up in a long arch.

3. After a long, full extension, the left elbow finally collapses.

FINISH POSITION

1. This is the only natural phase of the golf swing. Simply put, if you swing out correctly, you will probably have a good finish position. If you swing across the ball, you will finish somewhere over your left shoulder.

2. Swing out!!! Then let the hands "float" up.

3. *Don't pull* the club up! Swing out and let the momentum of the swing bring your hands and club up. Let the hands

come up as a *result* of the swing...not because you *pulled* them up.

4. Left side is "bowed" out - with the weight on the *outside* of the left foot. The left foot should "roll" out with the follow'-through. *Do not* allow your left foot to spin out or twist away from its original position.

5. Right side is relaxed.

6. Grip is still firm and the hands are high.

That is the swing. It can be so complicated yet so fluidly simple. It will determine your degree of success and fun in the game of golf.

Chapter 4

APPLYING THE SWING

TO YOUR CLUBS

A correctly hit shot...with club face absolutely square at impact and passing out straight at the target...will produce a straight ball with backspin. These are rare shots. Most shots will have a left-to-right or right-to-left spin to them.

With the irons, the longer the club...the smaller the face and hitting surface...therefore the more difficult to hit squarely...and the more likelihood of producing a spinning ball, which will curve away from the intended target. The easiest club to use is the #7 iron. This is the club to use in practice - when correcting a fault or working on a problem phase of the swing. A #5 iron is second best.

With woods - you are hitting the longest clubs in your set. The farther you are away from anything - the more skill needed to produce good results. Your woods may feel awkward and clumsy... because of their length...until you practice enough with them.

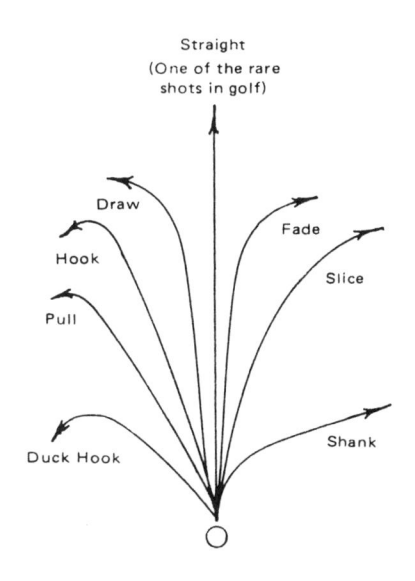

Straight
(One of the rare shots in golf)

Draw
Hook
Pull
Duck Hook
Fade
Slice
Shank

Discussion

"We strongly recommend that most men rarely, if every, use the #1 wood (driver). About 90% of men golfers swing *across* the ball. With a #1 wood, the club face puts a strong spin on the ball...producing a beautiful, but demoralizing, curve to the right. This is called a "slice", which is the scourge of golf. A #3 wood is easier to use. It captures the ball better on the clubface-producing less spin. Even though the #1 wood is supposed to hit the ball 15 yards farther...the average guy *will hit the #3 wood farther* because he will hit it better. What most golfers do not realize is that the finest players in the world *do not* use their drivers on "tight" holes...or in tense situations...or when they do not feel right.

Women are more relaxed and more flexible and less prone to swing across the ball. Most women should use the #1 wood off the tee.

In the final analysis, no one really cares what club(s) you used in your round. The only thing that counts is how many times you have hit the ball."

Discussion

"IN A ROUND OF GOLF, USE THE CLUBS WHICH ARE WORKING THE BEST FOR YOU. The place to develop skill and confidence with your tougher clubs is on the practice range and not on the course."

TAKING DIVOTS

You may set the ball up on a tee for the first shot of each hole. After that, each shot will be hit *out* of grass (or sand). In a correctly hit grass shot, the club is *descending* as it makes first contact with the ball. The ball is hit...and the club continues into the grass before it starts up. If ground conditions are not too hard, it is desirable to cut out a piece of sod...called a "divot". (This divot must be picked up...placed back in its original position and stepped down.) You will not take divots with fairway woods...only with irons. Women are very reluctant to hit down into the grass...which is why they tend to" top" so many shots. YOU MUST HIT DOWN...TO GET THE BALL UP! As soon as you discover this...you will hit better shots.

PRACTICE SUGGESTIONS

1. Warm-up and loosen up first.

2. Start all practice sessions with half swings...pitching strokes with the wedge or #9 iron. Next ...hit some full swing short irons, then some full swing middle irons and longer irons. Next...fairway woods (the least practiced shot in golf... except for sand shots.) Finally, hit some tee shots with the club you intend to use off the tee.

3. Have a purpose...a reason... for every practice swing and shot! Pick a direction, and a landing area for each shot. Train yourself to take a mental picture of where your shot will land...picture a beautiful golf shot each time...no matter how you are hitting. Or - work on a particular phase in your swing...a trouble area. Keep *one* thought in mind for several swings at a time.

4. *Learn the range of your clubs.* Knowing your hitting ability will make club selection more reliable when playing. You will develop judgment in club selection...only after you have hit many *good* shots in practice.

Most golf courses have 150 yard markers on par 4 and par 5 holes. These markers are 150 yards away from the center of the green. Men should know exactly what club they need for 150 yards, including the roll, under normal ground and wind conditions. Women should know what club they need for 100 yards - including the roll. Then, remember, in a full set you have a 10 yard difference between clubs...and 20 yards per club in a basic set. (e.g., if you get 150 yards with a #5 iron with a good hit...then you can expect 130 with a #7...160 with #4...170 with a #3...etc.)

PROBLEMS AND CORRECTIONS

Every golfer in the world will mishit the ball occasionally...and experience bad shots. If you *regularly* hit bad shots...with a definite pattern to them...the following chart will give you corrective suggestions to try in practice.

52   GOLF: From Tee to Green

Problem	Possible Cause	Try This
Slicing (LEFT HANDERS NOTE: Your "slices" will be to the left and your "hooks" will be to the right.)	Swinging across the ball.	Check your grip. Be sure V's point to right ear.
	Clubface open at impact.	Swing from inside out. Think of your hands coming in close to right hip on the way to the ball.
	Starting downswing with the hands.	Work on the practice suggestions in the impact area phase of the swing listed in this chapter.
Hooking	Grip rotated too far under ... to the right ...with left hand or both hands.	Check your grip. Be sure V's point to right ear. Open right-hand ...palm should face the target...not up.
	Clubface "hooded" or facing left at address.	Check clubface alignment. The bottom edge (sole) of club should be perpendicular to the line across toes.
	Backswing too "flat"... hands too low at the top of swing...much like a baseball swing	Check top of swing position. Hands should be high, with backs of knuckles pointing up.
Topping	Swing across the ball.	Swing squarely out through the ball.
	Coming off the ball too soon.	Hit down through the ball.
	Not shifting weight to left side as you swing through.	Shift weight over laterally as you swing to ball.
	Collapsing left arm at impact.	Review impact area suggestions.
Hitting Behind Ball	Picking club up on backswing.	Club should come away from ball low and straight.
	Too flat of a backswing.	Check top of swing position. Hands should be high and up.
	Weight on right foot too long.	Shift weight over laterally as you hit the ball.
	Dipping head in backswing.	Keep head steady throughout swing.

Applying the Swing 53

Problem	Possible Cause	Try This
Smothering or Scuffing	Dipping head in backswing.	Keep head steady throughout swing.
	Swaying out to right in backswing.	On backswing, weight should be on inside of right foot.
Lack of Distance	Not enough practice to develop a skillful, efficient swing.	Practice the fundamentals and mechanics of the swing as much as possible. (Be sure your teacher has pointed out the errors in your swing so that you practice with a purpose in mind.)
	Swinging across the ball.	
	Swaying to right on backswing.	Keep weight on inside of right foot on backswing, and kick the right knee into the swing.
	Need more strength in muscles used.	Any exercise program which will enhance total fitness...will help the golf swing. Ask your teacher for special exercises designed to develop a stronger golf swing.
	Breaking wrists too soon, causing a pick up of the club with the hands.	Keep wrists firm through the ball.
	Too upright of a backswing ... causing a *chopping* motion at the ball.	Take club back low from ball.
	Ball played back too far in stance when teed-up, or set up high in grass.	Play ball up toward left foot whenever it is on tee...or setting up high in grass. Ball may be teed too high.
Shanking	Too close or too far from ball at address.	RELAX!!! Check the basics in the address position.
	Grip loosened during course of swing.	RELAX...and work it out.
	Weight on toes in address, rather than back toward heels.	

Discussion

" A shank is an ugly...completely demoralizing shot. The real danger is that we fear repeating the shot...tense up...and, can very well do it over and over again. It can become a mental thing...golfers call it a disease...when it becomes a persistent problem."

APPLYING THE SWING TO THE SHORT GAME

Once off the tee - depending on your situation or "lie", and on the distance remaining to the flag, you will have a choice of 13 full-swing hitting clubs with a ten yard per club differential. In a "beginner" or "basic" set, you will choose from 6 hitting clubs with a 20 yard difference between clubs.

There comes a point(s) in the play of each hole when you do not need a full swing from any of your clubs. This is called the SHORT GAME...and includes *pitching...chipping...and putting.*

PITCHING

When you are close enough to the green that no matter how short a club you use...you cannot take a full swing. You now want a high lofted or "lob" shot onto the green...from where you will putt the ball into the cup.

Discussion

"Some people will make a whole new ball game out of pitching and chipping...making you feel as though you need to learn an entirely different swing. There is only one golf swing!...with 13 different tools to use. The only time in the golf game the swing significantly changes is when you putt. The basic mechanics and fundamentals are the same for all full swing shots. In pitching and chipping you use the same swing...but shorten the swing...swing only as hard as you think you need to for the distance left to the flag. How hard do you swing? No one can tell you this. It is a skill and a "feel" that comes only from practice. Hold your club a little shorter...perhaps put your feet closer together...or use an open stance if you wish. *Look* at where you want the ball to land on the green...and try to pitch the ball up to that spot".

You will pitch mostly with a #7 iron...#9 iron...or wedge. The first fundamental you must learn in pitching is to understand how each club will react...when hit properly:

A pitch with a #7 iron will travel in the air one-half the distance between you and the cup and roll the remaining distance on a flat green.

A pitch with a #9 iron will travel about two-thirds the distance between you and the cup and roll the remaining distance. (A wedge will elevate the pitch shot more and roll less.)

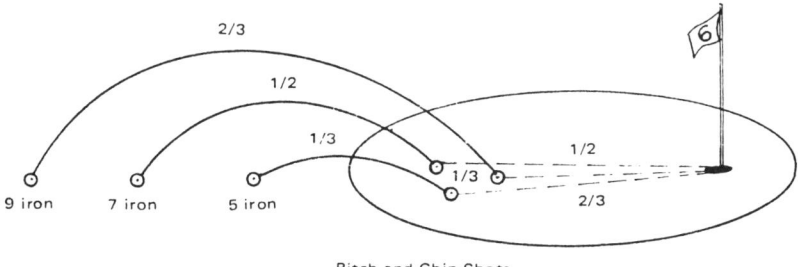

Pitch and Chip Shots

Discussion

"We all wonder in amazement how the pros make the ball stick...and even roll back after hitting the green with short clubs. They can do this for two reasons: First, they have fine golf swings...and when short irons are hit with proper swings, a lot of backspin is created. Secondly, they play the finest golf courses in the world, with beautiful greens which promote more backspin. (A course will devote two years of special maintenance in preparation for the one week the Pro Tour plays it.)"

CHIPPING

This is a short shot from just off the edge of the green which rolls up to the cup. A #5 iron is the most commonly used club here. If you are on the apron...or "frog's hair" (collar around the green)...use your putter. (Some low budget courses do not cut aprons around their greens...they go directly from fairway to green.)

Further Pitch and Chip Tips

1. After more experience, practice these with your weight on the left foot throughout the swing. This will help keep you steady, and create more backspin.

2. Keep your wrists *firm* as they pass through the shot. Think of the back of the left hand swinging out to the flag.

3. Your target in pitching and chipping is close and directly in front of you (the flag). As you pitch through...*reach* for the flag.

Discussion

"Every golfer, regardless of ability can develop skills in the short game. The mechanics of the swing are more simple and there is less chance for error. Pitch and chip shots are truly stroke savers for most golfers. Keep in mind that the fine players are hitting the greens from far out in the fairway or off the tee on par 3 holes. Therefore they are putting for *birdies* on most holes. The average gofer rarely hits the greens in *regulation*...(1 stroke on par 3's, 2 strokes on par 4's and 3 on par 5's)...hence is pitching or chipping to most greens. For lower scores...work on those short game skills."

PUTTING

Putting is the simplest part of the game...if you learn to relax and become realistic about putting. You are on the green...and, using a club designed for the purpose...will roll the ball toward...and into the cup. It is far easier to develop a fair degree of skill in putting than in any other phase of golf. The mechanics of the swing are the simplest...and the emphasis is on a comfortable, relaxed position.

Discussion

"This is the only stroke in golf in which the swing changes significantly. We do not shift the weight back and through the stroke...and we do not need a firm left arm. We stroke and *caress* the ball rather than hit it or swing at it.

Every putt cannot possibly roll in...no matter how much you study it. There may be a million blades of grass between your ball and the cup.. If a significant number are matted...or pointed the wrong way...your putt will be influenced. Be sensible...*relax*...you will miss some *easy* putts (which will be maddening)...but you will also make many putts. Relax...practice a sound, consistent putting stroke...learn to size-up your putts...and *practice!* Your head will be your own worst enemy. If you *think* you cannot putt well...then you will not! Research proves that...even though the physical effort is at a minimum...putting causes a much higher heart rate than any full swinging shot."

To become a good putter...you must:

1. Develop a sound consistent, *confident* putting stroke.

2. Develop good judgment in *sizing up* putts.

3. Practice...practice...practice!

Discussion

"Settle for one style...one which feels good to *you*...if it is basically correct...stay with it! In putting, there is a great leeway in styles...and you'll see some weird ones! Don't be influenced by odd styles...these people are hoping for some kind of miracle. *We create our own miracles* by developing confidence...a personal, comfortable style...and *practicing!*

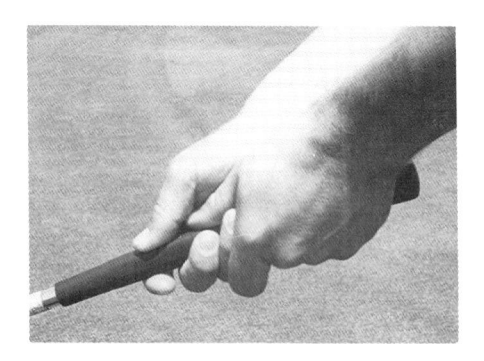

FUNDAMENTALS OF PUTTING

Grip

We change the grip. Except for special effect shots the fine players use...this is the only time we change the grip. Point both thumbs straight down the shaft...to square up the hands. (Most putters are made with a flat surface on top as a reminder to "square-up".) Use a *reverse-overlap* grip...with the forefinger of the left hand resting on the right hand underneath. A putt is a delicate, *finesse* stroke. If you are right-handed, you will have more feel...and impart more skill with your right hand dominating the stroke...so we weaken the left hand by reversing the grip.

Stance

Feet comfortably apart. A square stance makes more sense for most golfers...because it gives you a guideline (line across the toes) to use. If you feel more comfortable...and confident, open or close your stance slightly. Keep the weight on your left foot. Do not shift back and through as you stroke. Line the ball up on a line just inside your left heel. (More experienced golfers will vary this line with uphill and downhill putts...uphill with the ball played forward toward the left...and downhill back toward the middle.

The Stroke

Keep head and eyes down over the ball. Keep putter square to the line of the putt...and low along the grass as you stroke. Stroke smoothly *through* the ball, keeping the putter face square.

Judgment

Looking over or "sizing up" a putt before you stroke will help you determine the line...and give you an idea of the length of the putt. Look at the putt from a side view...and then kneel down behind the ball and study the path between your ball and the cup. Uphill...downhill...sidehill...wet...dry...all these factors will influence a putt...and must be taken into account.

Discussion

"The fine players study a putt from the side...from the hole to the ball...and then from the ball to the hole. Some may lay flat on the green to get a *worm's eye view* of the terrain. Some people will think you are wasting time...or *hot dogging*...in sizing up your putt. Since only one person at a time may putt, look your putt over while waiting your turn. You will...perhaps...putt fewer times and actually *save* time in the long run.

Get a comfortable position and style...size up your putts...and, with practice...you will do it more easily by developing better judgment in your putting."

Grain

The "grain" of a green will also influence putts. Particularly in Northern climates, creeping bent grass is primarily used in building greens. The grass on each green will have a pattern to it...it will tend to grow in *one* direction. Rolling a ball into the tips of the grass *against the grain* will take more effort than putting the ball *with the grain*. On a flat putt, across the grain...the ball will curve in the direction of the grain.

To pick out the grain on a green:

1. The grass will always grow towards the brightest direction...towards lakes and open fairways...and *away* from woods, hills and mountains. So you will get a clue as you walk up to the green.

2. Verify your clue by looking at the top of the hole. A tool is used to cut out the hole for the cup. The grass will grow over one edge of the cup...and away from the opposite edge...which should give you the "grain".

If this is confusing...do not be concerned. Many golfers play a lifetime and do not take the grain of the green into account.

Practice...practice. Your skills in putting will develop more rapidly than any other phase of the game. It is the simplest stroke in golf. There are many golfers who are poor players—but good putters. You have more opportunities to practice putting than any other phase of golf. Every course has a practice putting green...usually located near the first tee. You should practice while waiting for your group to tee-off. Take a few balls and your putter and go to any public golf course...and practice at your leisure. There is no fee charged for this.

APPLYING THE SWING TO TROUBLE SHOTS

Try as we might to put the ball where we want it to go... it will sometimes end up in unusual situations...which adds an additional challange to our golf skills. (We said it was an interesting game.)

All golf courses are designed to penalize errant shots. The penalties may be in the form of "penalty strokes"...or more difficult shots to challenge your skills. Learning what adjustments have to be made...and developing the skills needed to these situations will make the game more enjoyable as well as boost your confidence as a player.

UNEVEN LIES

There are four different types of uneven lies which will require adjustments in your swing...and in your thinking.

Uphill Lie

1. Play the ball toward higher foot (left).

2. Aim slightly to right of target. This stance will produce a right to left shot.

3. Because the loft of the club is increased as you set it down, use one club longer than the shot calls for.

4. Take several practice swings to get used to the difference in balance. (Weight is on the right foot here.) Swing *with* the slope.

Downhill Lie

1. Play the ball toward higher foot (right).

2. Aim slightly to right of target...this situation produces a left to right spin on the ball.

3. Use the club you would normally hit for the distance involved here (even though the loft of the club is decreased...the fade will negate the additional distance we may expect).

4. Take several practice swings. Weight is on the left leg. Get used to swinging with the slope.

Applying the Swing 63

Sidehill Lie (with the ball above the feet)

1. Shorten grip on club.

2. Play ball in center of stance.

3. This set-up will produce a right to left spin...so aim slightly to right of target.

4. Take of few practice swings.

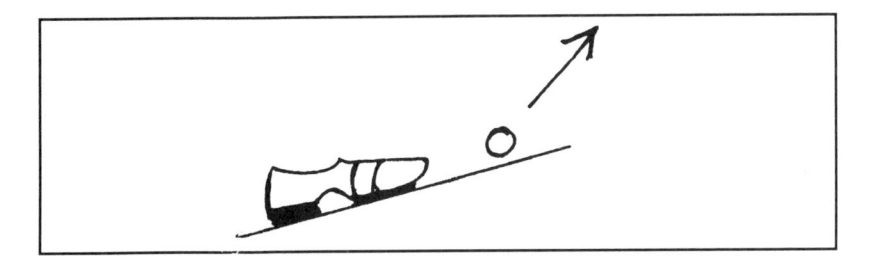

Sidehill Lie (with ball below the feet)

This is one of the most difficult shots in golf.
1. Use one club longer.

2. Play ball in center of stance.

3. Flex knees a little more.

4. Since this set-up will produce a left to right fade...aim slightly left.

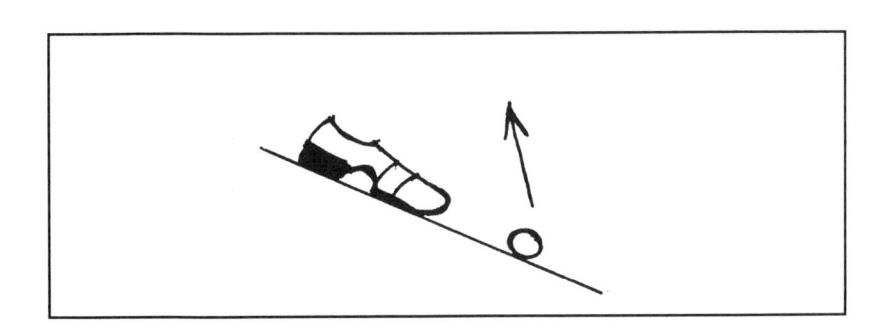

HITTING OUT OF HEAVY GRASS (ROUGH)

1. Good strategy would be to sacrifice distance. Your first concern should be to get out of the situation and back on the fairway. When you become more experienced, you may gamble more.

2. If the grass is not too thick...#4 or #5 woods are good clubs to use if distance is needed...or one of the new style "trouble clubs" with runners on the sole will get the ball out and up mrie easily.

3. Use a more upright backswing...and follow-through to pick the ball out. In a normal swing there will be too much grass between the club face and ball at impact...reducing distance.

4. Do *not* overswing. Swing in your normal tempo. Do a little thinking and then trust your club...and your swing.

SAND SHOTS

By rule, you *cannot* ground your club (touch the sand with your club)...except in the shot itself...Penalty - 2 strokes.

Discussion

"The pros do not mind playing out of sand traps. In fact, many prefer sand shots to some grass lies. They have developed special techniques for all types of sand shots...through many hours of practice. Unless you are a member of a private club which has a practice trap...you will rarely have the opportunity to practice trap shots. Instead of trying a rather radical change in basic swing fundamentals...use one of the other following techniques suggested."

Pro Style for Hitting Out of Sand

Open stance...settle feet firmly into the sand...aim slightly left of flag. Pick out a spot 1/2 to 1 inch behind the ball and swing *across* the target line in an "outside-in" stroke. (This is the only shot in golf where the ball is not contacted first). The idea is to "peel out" a layer of sand under the ball with a lot of force...which pops (or "blasts") the ball up and out. The pros will use a sand wedge here...although a pitching wedge or #9 iron may work.

OTHER TECHNIQUES

If you have a good lie...or are in hard-packed sand...you may try picking the ball out cleanly with whatever lofted club you need to get over the lip of the trap.

If the lip is shallow and sloped away from you...try a "Texas Wedge"...a putter...and roll the ball out.

Using a pitching wedge or #9 iron...*hood* or close the club face slightly and swing *hard*. Sand offers more resistance than grass. Swing hard enough to think of hitting the ball over the flag.

If the ball is partly buried...*fried egg* lie...hood your club face over and swing very *hard*.

Fairway traps will require full swings. Choose a club which will give you enough loft to get over the lip...then think about the distance involved. (A #5 wood works well out of traps.)

> **Discussion**
>
> "Sand trap shots are demeaning and demoralizing. Average golfers have little confidence in them...which adds tension to the swings reducing hope for skillful shots. Confidence comes *only* from practice. (If you are keeping the faith...a little prayer for divine help may relax you a bit in your sand trap.)"

WIND SHOTS

Pluck a little grass and flip it into the air before each shot. The wind will influence the flight of the ball. The more lofted the club - the greater the effect of the wind on the shot.

With the Wind

1. Use less club than the shot calls for.

2. Play the ball up toward the left foot.

3. On a tee shot, tee up higher than usual...and lean the tee back a bit.

4. In a pitching situation, use a pitch and run with a #7 iron whenever possible.

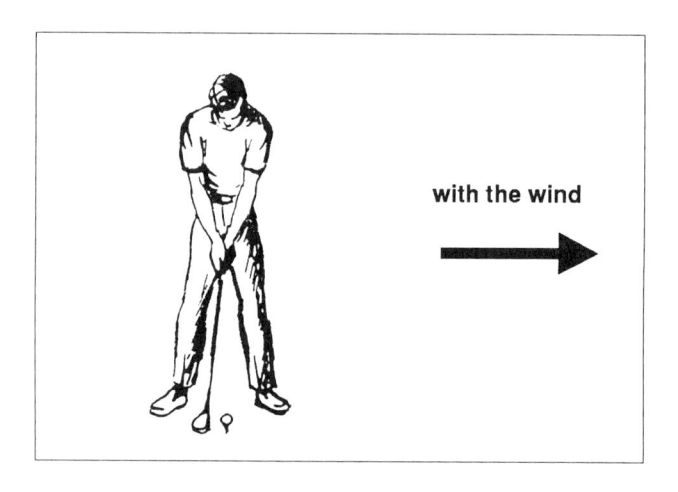

with the wind →

Into the Wind

1. Use one or two clubs longer, depending on the velocity of the wind.

2. Play the ball back in the middle of the stance.

3. Widen your stance a bit.

4. Shorten your grip on the club.

5. Keep the club low to the ground on the backswing.

6. Hit into the ball *boldly*...but do not overswing. Expect less roll to the ball.

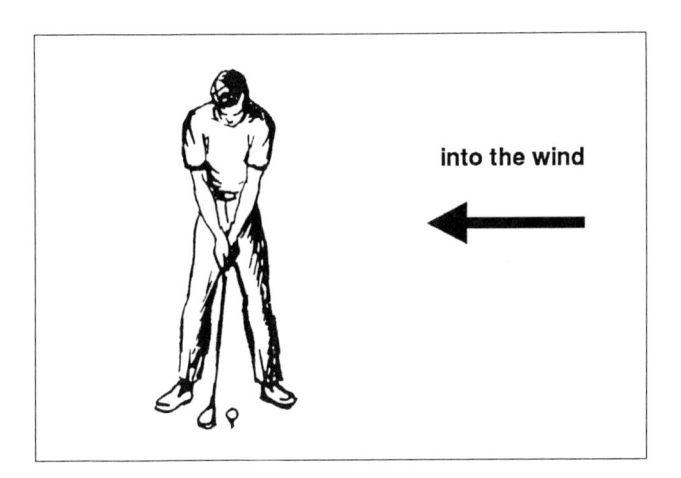

into the wind

Crosswind Shots

1. Use one club longer.

2. Turn the direction of your stance and swing slightly *into* the wind.

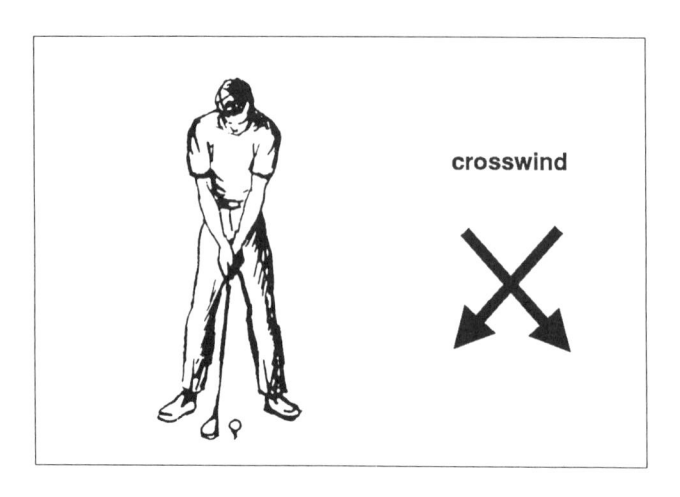

WET CONDITIONS

Playing in the rain and wet conditions can be fun...if you are dressed properly and are equipped with an umbrella and a large towel. (It *does* rain on a golf course...but you only get wet *once!*) Your shots will not bounce or roll as much and the approach shots to the green will stick better. Many golfers score better in wet conditions.

1. Play a more deliberate game.

2. Use at least one club more in your shot-making.

3. Widen your stance slightly...and shorten the grip for better control.

4. Swing boldly...but do not overswing.

5. With pitches, play more bold, lofted shots than pitch and run.

6. Keep your club grips dry...and wipe the club face after each shot.

COLD WEATHER

Dress in thin layers of knit clothing...avoid bulky sweaters and jackets. Thermal ski underwear is a good idea. Wear a light, wind-proof jacket over all. A knit ski cap...or "watch" cap are good.

If you are going to play in cold weather regularly, you should buy special winter golf gloves...or simply buy a matching regular golf glove for your other hand. Hand warmers...using lighter fluid...are available. Use a lower compression ball.

HOT WEATHER

Dress in loose, porous, light-colored clothing. Wear a brimmed hat. Carry a clean towel to dry eyes and hands. In extreme heat - use your umbrella. Avoid alcoholic and carbonated beverages...as well as coffee. Cool water at regular intervals is the best idea. (Drinking water is available at various points around the course.) While waiting for others to hit...stay in the shade as much as possible. Shorten the grip on the club for all shots.

70   GOLF: From Tee to Green

Chapter 5

PLAYING THE GAME

You have made arrangements for a game with a few friends. Before you leave, you should call the golf course you wish to play to see if you need starting times...or if they have a tournament or league play scheduled. The least crowded times are mid-morning and mid-afternoon. An excellent and comfortable time to play is early evening. If you are a beginner or have little experience on a course, pick a friend who knows the game and has played before...and tell that person that you are new to the game. Hopefully, it is a good friend who will be empathetic, patient and helpful.

Call for weather information so that you may dress appropriately. Now it's off to the golf course!

IN THE CLUBHOUSE

You will change your shoes in the car and usually come dressed for play. (If you play at a private country club, you will bring a change of clothes with you in a gripper bag and dress in the locker room.)

Do not bring your clubs in to the clubhouse or pro shop. Leave them outside in the club racks or railings you will see outside the door.

Buy your ticket (or greens fee), get a scorecard and pencil and tighten your golf spikes if needed. Decide if you will carry your bag or rent a pull cart. (Motorized golf carts are fun...and may be rented...two players to a cart.)

Check to be sure you have about six balls, several tees, ball markers and a ball mark repair tool.

If the course is crowded, report to the "starter" at the first tee and list your group with him. If there is no starter, find out how many groups are ahead of you and know which group you will follow. Some courses will have a ball rack on the first tee in which you will place a ball representing your group. Your group's turn will come up when your ball appears. (Be sure you remember the name and number of the ball you placed in the rack.)

When the course is busy, they will expect you to play in groups of four or "foursomes." If you are alone - or with a friend or two - the starter will round out your foursome by putting others in with you. If the course is not busy, you may play a twosome, threesome - or alone if you wish. A group of five will be slow - you should ask permission in the clubhouse if there will be five in your group.

While you await your turn on the tee, warm-up, and then practice putting on the practice green, which should be near by.

PLAYING CONDITIONS

Decide in your group under what playing conditions you will play. Depending on the weather and condition of the course, there are three basic kinds of playing conditions to consider.

SUMMER RULES

Under summer rules, you cannot move the ball or improve your lie anywhere...except in penalty situations or "free drop" situations which we will come to in this chapter. You will generally play summer rules at private clubs only...and only when a sign near the first tee indicates "Summer Rules Today". (Private clubs do not get the traffic public fee courses do and are better able to keep their fairways in good shape so that the balls set up well.)

WINTER RULES

These are strictly local rules...played on public or fee courses...and vary with the locale. Some allow you to improve your lie by rolling the ball with your club...a distance of 6"...and not nearer the hole you are playing. Some allow a club length distance relief from the original lie...again not toward the hole you are playing. Generally, this is allowed in your own fairway only...although some will play "winter rules" all over except in hazards. Very liberal rules may allow a hand set of the ball after movement.

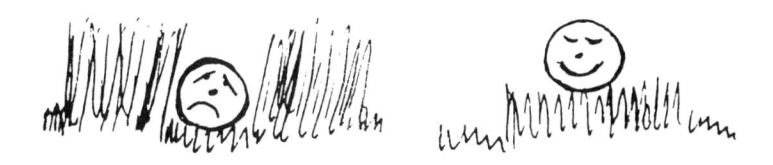

PREFERRED LIES OR "PICK-N-CLEAN"

When playing conditions are unusually bad such as in early spring and after heavy rains, you may decide to play under preferred lie rules. Here, you may put a marker under your ball...lift it...clean it off...and hand set it...no nearer the hole.

A "plugged ball" rule is always in effect. Anytime (except in a hazard) the ball is submerged or *plugged*...you may lift it ...clean it...and hand set it.

If you are playing in a tournament or league, a rules committee will decide under what rules the course will be played that day. In sociable golf...you simply decide among yourselves.

The United States Golf Association does not sanction "winter rules" or "preferred lies"...except in extreme conditions. (These people obviously do not play public fee golf courses.) These are strictly local rules...which take precedence over USGA Rules.

HANDICAPS

There is a rating system in golf which equalizes play in friendly games, or in tournament and league play. If you play a course regularly or play in a league, you will be asked to turn in several scores early in the season to a committee...who will determine your "handicap". The system used may range from a sophisticated, closely-supervised procedure at some clubs - to a more simplified version. There are even several "one day" handicap formulas used in some tournaments.

A SCORECARD

Scorecards and golf pencils are available in the pro shop or office...and usually in a box near the first tee.

A scorekeeper is chosen for your group and all players are listed on the card. (An unwritten rule in sociable golf is "high score on the first hole keeps score for the round.")

Besides the spaces for scores on each hole, a scorecard will provide needed information such as:

1. The yardage, par and handicap rating of each hole.
   Yardages will be shown from the red (ladies') tees, white (mens') and blue (championship or tiger) tees. (Some courses are now introducing "gold" tees for senior golfers.)

   Mens' par and ladies' par for each hole, based on the length of the holes.

   Handicap Rating. After building a course, the pro or a selected committee of good players will play the course and rate each hole in degree of difficulty in comparison to the other holes on the course. Therefore, if a hole has a #1 listed in the handicap column, it is considered to be the most difficult, on that course. Handicap columns are used to designate the holes on which "strokes are given" in events using established player handicaps and in friendly wagers. (Rick has a handicap rating of 7...and Jim is rated at 10. In a game, Rick must give Jim 3 strokes in medal play...or one stroke on each of the holes rated, 1, 2, and 3 in the handicap column on the scorecard in a match play game.)

2. A scorecard will also list the "out-of-bounds" places on the course...and a set of Local Rules. Local rules are set up by the golf course operators and *supersede* USGA rules.

3. A scorecard may also list reminders for courteous and business-like play.

GROSS SCORE AND NET SCORE

Gross score in a round of golf is your total actual score, counting all swings at the ball. *Net score* is your gross score...minus your handicap.

Playing the Game

U.S.G.A. RULES TO GOVERN ALL PLAY

LOCAL RULES:
All current year local options as recommended and adopted by the Cleveland District Golf Association and its member clubs.

OUT OF BOUNDS:
Marked by white stakes. Left on # 3, 4, 5, 6, 7, 10, 11, 12, 13, 14 and 15. Back of 11 and 14.

WATER HAZARDS:
Crossing = 2, 5, 7, 8, 9, 11, 12 and 17. Parallel hazard on right of # 17, beyond creek crossing is marked by red stakes.

SWALES:
To be played as rough. Casual water rule to apply. Left on # 2, Right on # 13, 14, 15 and 17.

BALL:
Lying in drain covers, sprinkler heads, pipes, areas marked 'GROUND UNDER REPAIR', staked and/or wired trees, maintenance roads and cart paths. May be dropped, 2 club lengths, not nearer the hole—NO PENALTY!

PRACTICE ON GREENS, TEES AND TRAPS IS FORBIDDEN!
SUMMER GOLF UNLESS OTHERWISE POSTED!

- SMOOTH THE SAND TRAPS.
- REPLACE TURF.
- WHEN LOST, WAVE NEXT GROUP THROUGH.
- KEEP CARTS AWAY FROM TEES AND GREENS.

Phone 946-8798

38000 Lake Shore Blvd. • Willoughby, Ohio 44094

Championship (BLUE TEES)	425	568	134	328	402	442	177	479	425	3380
Regular (WHITE TEES)	403	548	125	304	393	425	150	454	413	3215
HOLES	1	2	3	4	5	6	7	8	9	**OUT**
MEN'S PAR	4	5	3	4	4	4	3	5	4	36
HANDICAP STROKES	5	9	17	15	7	3	11	13	1	

MATCHES WE / THEY

1.
2.
3.
4.

LADIES' PAR	4	5	3	4	4	4	3	5	4	36
Ladies Yardage	352	465	125	287	344	372	142	425	360	2872
HANDICAP STROKES	11	3	17	15	9	5	13	7	1	

SCORER _____ ATTESTED _____

Championship (BLUE TEES)	467	366	183	372	347	386	165	545	502	3333	3380	6713		
Regular (WHITE TEES)	456	360	172	360	325	376	148	535	472	3204	3215	6419	HANDICAP	NET SCORE
HOLES	10	11	12	13	14	15	16	17	18	**IN**	**OUT**	**TOT**		
MEN'S PAR	4	4	3	4	4	4	3	5	5	36	36	72		
HANDICAP STROKES	2	12	10	14	16	4	18	6	8					

MATCHES WE / THEY

LADIES' PAR	4	4	3	4	4	4	3	5	5	36	36	72		
Ladies Yardage	396	354	149	320	280	318	141	465	412	2835	2872	5707		
HANDICAP STROKES	2	12	10	14	16	6	18	4	8					

DATE _____

In sociable golf...and/or in tournament or league play...you will have both - a medal (gross) event and a net event (using handicaps). The better players will win the low gross events...and everyone has a shot at the low net prizes.

MATCH PLAY OR MEDAL PLAY

Competitive golf may be played in two styles - Match play or Medal. Match play is a won, lost or tie - hole by hole competition...regardless the number of strokes each hole is won or lost by. In medal play, the difference between opponents in total strokes for the round...determines the winner. (Amy scores a 6 on the first hole and Beth has a 4. Beth is one up match play and two up medal.)

RULES OF GOLF

Golf has a definite set of rules under which the game is played. These are established USGA Rules...superseded only by any Local Rules. There are also rules of etiquette...which should be known and observed by all players. (In friendly, "sociable" golf, the game may be played under more lenient versions of official rules. These are not legal in serious play - but are seen in casual play.)

Your objective is to hit the ball straight and true. This is not always possible. Golf penalizes errant, off-target shots either by the addition of "penalty" strokes...or by more difficult situations from which to hit. Golf rules are not meant to be obstacles, but are written to actually *help the player*...if known and fully understood.

Let's play a golf hole together...and look at some of the basic rules for play and rules of courtesy which may be involved. Also a few suggestions to make the game more enjoyable and rewarding for all.

THE TEE

1. Never bring carts or sets of clubs on to a tee...just a ball, tee and the club you intend to use.

2. No two players in your group should play exactly the same ball. Balls to be used should be identified on the first tee.

3. The order of hitting off the first tee is by random choice. After the first hole and thereafter, lowest score hits first, second lowest hits second, etc. In a mixed group, the women will hit first (according to scores) and then the men. If the red markers are a considerable distance ahead of the mens' tees, the men would hit first and then the group would move up to the ladies' markers.

4. You *do not* tee off until all players in the group ahead of you are out of range of one of your *good* shots.

5. When someone is hitting, you stand quietly a distance behind the hitter. Watch every shot in your group (especially any wild hits) so that you have a good idea where every shot goes. If everyone does, this, you will waste less time looking for lost balls.

Discussion

"We have an unwritten rule in sociable golf: *No one is allowed to laugh...until after a shot!*

At the first tee (with several other people watching) you may experience first tee jitters. We all do. This is a normal feeling and is to be expected. If you feel paranoid and feel the others are watching with scorn...forget it! Their turns are coming up...and they have nothing but sympathy for you"

6. When it is your turn, pick a level spot between the two markers. By rule, you may not tee ahead of the markers...or more than two club lengths behind them.

7. If using a wood, set the tee so that 1/2 the ball is above the top of the club face. With irons, set the tees lower to the ground.

8. Use the ball to press the tee into the ground - not your thumbs.

9. After the hit, *watch your ball* carefully until it stops rolling or disappears from sight. If it disappears, line-up your shot with a tree or bush...or other distinguishing landmark...have a good idea where your ball is at all times. (Do not lose sight of the ball to look for a tee...the ball is more valuable.)

FAIRWAY TO THE GREEN

1. After you have all hit, pick-up your equipment and move smartly toward your ball. *Never* walk out in front of anyone hitting a shot. Keep walking to your ball...stopping to wait if someone in your group is in the same general line and will hit before you. The person farthest from the flag hits first...throughout the hole.

2. When waiting while someone else is hitting, the proper place to stand is facing the hitter...and slightly behind. If you are a considerable distance away or in another direction...simply keep moving on to your ball.

3. Keep your bag or cart with you and park them facing you while pondering your shot. Do not leave them a distance behind you and walk back and forth...or park them right at the ball so that you have to fuss with them after selecting your club.

4. In the hit, if you have cut out a divot (piece of sod) you are obliged to replace it. Leave your club to mark the hole...find the divot, replace it carefully and step it down around the edges.

5. Anytime you hit a ball towards someone - yell "FORE!" This is the national signal for a ball hit into your area...and one you must use when hitting at someone else.

> **Discussion**
>
> "Good players take divots with almost all iron shots. A well-played iron shot will cut out a divot. Women especially are reluctant to hit out of grass, which causes much of the topping. (If you feel badly because you think you are ruining the course's grass...carry a little grass seed with you.)"

BASIC RULES - TEE TO GREEN

Generally, there are one stroke and two stroke penalty situations covered by the official rules of golf. There are also situations from which you may move your ball - or get "relief" without penalty.

One Stroke Penalties

Lost Ball

If you lose a ball, you are obliged to go back to the original spot from which you hit that ball and hit another...adding one stroke in penalty. To save time, if you have hit into an area which looks like trouble, hit a second ball right then and there. This is called a "provisional" ball. (In sociable golf, many players drop another ball in the general area in which the original was lost...add a stroke...and continue play.) By rule you are allowed to take up to 5 minutes looking for a lost ball. If you do take this time allotment, you are obligated to allow the group behind you to play on through as you search.

Out of Bounds

Listed on the scorecard, and designated on the course by rows of short white stakes, there are out of bounds areas on every golf course. There is a one stroke penalty for hitting out. Hit a provisional ball if you think you may be outside the stakes. If your original is in...you must play it. If it is out, add a stroke and play the second ball. (In sociable golf, some golfers will bring the ball just inside where it went out...add a stroke, and keep playing.)

Unplayable Lie

If you hit into a situation anywhere on the course that you cannot play out of...or choose not to play out of...you may declare an unplayable lie. Now you have three options:

1. Move the ball two club lengths from the spot...in any direction except toward the hole you are playing...and drop it for a one stroke penalty.

2. You may go back to the original spot you played the ball from, add a stroke...and hit again.

3. Your third option is to take the ball and, keeping the trouble spot between you and the green, take it back as far as you wish, drop it, add a stroke, and keep playing.

Ball in a Water Hazard

If you hit into a creek or lake you are penalized one stroke. In dropping another ball, you must keep the "point of entry" of your shot into the hazard between you and the direction you are playing and drop anywhere along a line behind that spot. You also have the option - for the one stroke penalty - of going back to your original position prior to hitting into the hazard and playing another ball.

If you hit into a lateral hazard (when the water is parallel to the direction of the hole you are playing) you may drop the ball two club lengths in from the point of entry, add a penalty stroke and play from there. You also have the option of playing another shot from your original position.

Some courses and leagues have local versions of the water hazard rules. These would supersede the official rules.

Dropping the Ball

The correct manner in which to drop a ball...whether it is in a penalty situation or a "free drop" - is to measure out the awarded distance, extend the arm to the side - face the flag you are playing - and drop the ball being careful that it does not touch you on the way down. If the drop rolls into another bad situation...or closer to the hole...drop it again. After a second drop you are entitled to place it by hand.

You must play the course as it is. You may not pull, bend or remove anything that is growing. You may not stamp down the grass behind the ball. You cannot break branches...or have someone hold them while you hit.

You may remove loose natural impediments such as leaves, rocks, twigs...from all places except sand traps and water hazards. Artificial objects such as rakes, bottles, cans and paper may be removed from any place on the course - including hazards.

If your ball is cut...you may declare it unfit for play and replace it...with the approval of your opponents. Otherwise you may only change balls on a tee or on the green.

THE GREEN

On the green is where a rather stringent set of rules apply. Official rules, and rules of etiquette and fair play must be observed.

1. With your ball on the green, take your clubs to the back edge of the green - on the way to the next tee - and come out with your putter. Never set clubs on the green...or park carts near the edge.

2. Repair any ball mark your shot may have made in hitting the green. Small two-pronged tools for this purpose are available in pro shops and should be carried - or simply use a tee as a repair tool.

3. The person closest to the hole in your group is obligated to "attend" the flag on that hole. In attending the flag, stand at arm's length, with feet together and holding the cloth to keep it from fluttering. Keep your shadow away from the hole. Face the person farthest from the cup. The putter has the option of putting with the flag attended...or having it taken out. Generally, when all putters can see the hole from where they are...the flag is removed and laid down a distance from the hole. There is a *two stroke* penalty for striking the flagstick when putting from the green proper. The flag must be attended...or taken out.

4. *Do not* step in the line of any putt! Before the grass works its way back up, the putt may be deflected as it rolls

through. As you walk around the green, walk around the balls...or carefully *step over* the paths or lines of putts.

5. There is to be no talking, fidgeting or motion while someone is putting. You should be sizing up your putt while awaiting your turn. Keep your shadow away from the hole, and the line of a putt.

6. The person "away" putts first...and may continue putting until the ball drops into the cup...unless he or she must stand in the line of someone else's putt...then the ball should be marked...and the putting finished later.

7. Do not putt with another ball in your path. It should be marked. Good players usually mark *all* balls so as to leave no distractions for the putter. There is a *two stroke penalty* for striking another ball when putting. To mark a ball, place a small coin or plastic marker (available in pro shops)...behind and under the ball. (Many models of gloves have buttons which pop off and serve as markers.) If your marker will be directly in the line of the putt, use your putter head and place your marker a putter's head distance - laterally - away from the spot.

8. On par 3 holes...when the course is crowded...you are asked to "waive" up the group behind you. With all people in your group on the green...leave the flag in...step aside to the back of the green...and allow the people behind to hit their tee shots. While they are walking up, your group will putt out. If this rule is observed all over the course...play will be speeded up.

9. After everyone in your group has holed out, replace the flag and move quickly off the green and on to the next tee. *Do not* record scores on the green! Do it on the next tee.

10. If the ball is wedged between the flagstick and edge of the hole (in a shot from off the green)...the person whose shot it was must tilt the flagstick away so that the ball drops into the cup. If the ball pops out...it must be putted in... for another stroke.

FREE DROP SITUATIONS

There are a number of reasons and situations from which a ball may be moved without penalty. Some of these are:

1. Casual Water Rule - Water which is not intended to be there (such as puddles after a rain storm) creates casual water situations. You need not play out of or stand in casual water. You are allowed to take your ball out of the area - one club length away from the nearest point of relief - and drop it without penalty. On the green you do not putt through casual water. Using the flagstick, measure your distance from the cup and place your ball a like distance away in any direction you find a dry path to the hole.

2. Immovable Equipment - Any golf course equipment which interferes with your shot...entitles you to a free drop...one club length away...not nearer the hole. This includes benches, ball washers, hose couplings, cart paths, maintenance roads, etc.

3. If your ball is in a burrowing animal hole...or if the mound or residue earth interferes with your shot...you get a free drop...one club length not nearer the hole.

4. If your ball lands on the *wrong green*, you *must* drop the ball off the green and not nearer the green you're playing to.

5. Ground Under Repair - Golf course maintenance crews, who are supervised by a landscaping expert called a "greenskeeper, " are continually repairing and improving areas on the course. Areas currently being worked on are designated as "ground under repair." These are usually staked out...marked with signs...or ringed with white lime. You are entitled to a free drop from any such condition.

6. Newly planted trees are staked and supported with guide wires. You always drop away from staked trees. However, you *must* play out from under all non-staked trees and bushes...unless you choose to take a penalty stroke for moving from an unplayable lie.

MORE TWO STROKE PENALTIES

Grounding Club in Hazard

If your ball lies in a sandtrap...you may *not* touch the sand with your club...except in the actual swing at the ball. Enter the trap carefully...and address the ball without touching the sand.

If in a water hazard (creek or lake)...and your ball is playable on a bank...the same rule applies. You may not touch grass, pebbles or sticks when entering the hazard or in the address at the ball. Many courses now outline the hazard properly with rows of red stakes. Inside the stakes is considered hazard.

Unsportsmanlike Conduct

Many league and tournament rules committees impose a two stroke penalty rule for bad conduct such as foul language, club throwing and other acts of immature emotional outbursts. Rules committees reserve the right to assess two stroke penalties or disqualifications at their discretion.

Rules of etiquette and common courtesies are an integral part of golf. They are designed to enhance the enjoyment of the game for everyone and to protect the playing condition of the golf course.

Speed Up Play - Let's make a pitch here and now for faster play. There is currently a national campaign in effect among all organized golf organizations in the interest of faster play. One of

> **Discussion**
>
> The previous are but some of the basic rules for golf. We cannot cover them all here. If you intend to play serious golf...tournaments, league play, etc....you should carry an official USGA Rules Book in your bag. These are available in most pro shops.
> Colorful, illustrated pocket rules booklets are available at a nominal cost from the National Golf Foundation, 200 Castelwood Drive, North Palm Beach, Florida, 33404. These are *Easy Way to Learn Golf Rules* and are also available in wall chart form.

the only negative aspects to the game of golf is that a typical round takes too long to play. Many golfers take the fun out of the game for others by playing too slowly. Golf is meant to be played in a business-like manner. There is ample time during a round for socializing and observing the wonders of nature. But, all players should be *ready to hit* when it is their turn! And all players should *move smartly* between shots.

Playing time should not be longer than 2 - 2 1/2 hours for nine holes and 4 hours for eighteen.

If your group is playing slower than the group behind you...and there is a gap (room for them) ahead of you...you should allow the faster players through.

RULES OF SAFETY

Considering the great number of people playing golf, there are relatively few injuries. However, injuries in golf can be serious and we must be aware of the inherent dangers in the game...and be constantly alert. Most accidents in golf occur from carelessness...lack of knowledge...and because of intense concentration during play, which makes some people oblivious to danger. You have a responsibility for your own safety...and for the safety of all others on the course.

Always play with these *rules of safety* in mind:

1. Before you swing any club *anywhere* - be sure no one is near you.

2. Be aware of anyone swinging a club in your vicinity. Stay well out of the range of a golf swing.

3. Before you hit any shot, be sure the group ahead of you is well out of range of one of your best shots.

4. Never stand...or walk ahead...of any shot which may endanger you. A golf ball can take some weird and circuitous avenues of flight as you will see...or have seen.

5. Yell "Fore" if you hit a ball in anyone's direction. Duck and cover up if you hear "FORE" from anywhere!

6. When hitting near trees...take into account the possibility of ricochet shots.

7. In trouble situations, check for rocks and roots under your ball. These may damage your club in the swing. You may choose to declare an unplayable lie...if these cannot be removed without moving the ball.

8. When allowing faster groups to play through...or if your group is detained by a lost ball and you wave a group through...stand well aside the fairway - and perhaps behind a tree trunk - as they hit.

9. Never lick a golf ball. This is a habit we see occasionally. Fertilizers and pesticides are used regularly on the course...these are harmful to human beings. Ball washers - found at just about every tee - will keep your ball clean.

10. Foul Weather Play - Conditions on a golf course are extremely hazardous during *electrical* storms. *Use your head*!! If possible, suspend play and get back to the clubhouse before the storm breaks. The USGA has adopted a standard warning signal. Three short blasts on a siren to *discontinue* play...and a long siren signal to *resume* play. According to recently adopted rules you may stop play anytime you see lightning...whether there is a signal or not. If you suspend play with the intention of returning after the all-clear, mark the spot where your ball

lays as you would on the green. If you cannot make it back to the clubhouse, take these precautions:

a. Seek shelter in one of the strategically located shelter houses on the course.
b. Avoid tall trees or isolated trees. If there is no shelter house nearby, seek a stand of trees of relatively the same height.
c. Do not raise a metal-handled umbrella.
d. Avoid ridges, mounds or high places.
e. Leave your clubs a good distance away from you.
f. *Do not* walk down a fairway...you may draw lightning as would an isolated tree.
g. In *extremely violent* electrical storms, throw vanity to the wind...take off spiked shoes...keep your clubs about 50 yards away from you...do not use an umbrella ...and lie down in a depression of some sort.

Chapter 6

WHAT YOUR HEAD CAN DO FOR YOUR BODY

For many of you, this may be the most important chapter in the book. Even if you forsake golf - or give it only a token effort - it may be of benefit to you to give serious thought to the observations and reflections expressed here.

Golf is a complex game. There is much to learn and too much to remember. Percentage-wise, few people excel in golf. It takes more skill - developed through more hours of practice and individual instruction - to excel in golf than most popular games. The mechanics of a good golf swing are contrary to a comfortable, natural pattern of movement. Therefore the swing needs regular practice.

However, golf is a game even the unskilled, occasional player may enjoy greatly - if the mental approach is realistic and positive.

Golf is a mental game. Once the basic physical skills are learned and developed, up to 90% of the game becomes mental. Golf lends itself completely to the current emphasis on perhaps age-old theories concerning positive thinking...visual imagery...mental rehearsal..."mind over matter," etc. Let's take a look at how some of these theories apply to golf.

KNOW THYSELF

We are continually amazed at how little the human being knows about the human being. Having been students of human nature for many years...through many walks in life...we are obsessed with the old Quaker adage - "Know Thyself." This is perhaps the most valuable lesson we have to learn in life. All other pursuits seem secondary en route to a happy, fruitful life.

Nothing surprises us about the problems we humans have on earth. With all our intelligence...*we are so dumb about ourselves!*

Golfers are perfect examples of unrealistic, frustrated approaches to one of life's challenges. They exemplify how little we truly know about ourselves and each other.

Teaching golf these many years and working with thousands of people, it still is incredible to us that even intelligent, educated people lose sight of certain known basics about the human being. For instance:

1. We are born with varying degrees of ability - or "talent." Some are born with more than their fair share...and golf will be easier for these chosen few. Learn to accept your ability...whatever it is...you cannot change this. Don't put demands on yourself by setting unrealistic goals. Be honest with yourself...make the best of what you have...and with the degree to which you have *developed* your abilities. "It's not what you have - it's *what you do with it* that counts!"

2. At this point in history, there is only one way to gain skill...and that is through diligent practice...repeated rehearsal of the movements desired. The more practice...the greater the degree of skill developed. Your success in golf will be directly related to the amount of time devoted to worthwhile practice...tempered by your innate abilities. We are greatly impressed with the ridiculous ease with which pros hit out of sand traps. Pro golfers spend hours practicing out of sand traps. How many hours *do you* spend in trap practice? Pros practice at least an hour before each round...we average 5 - 10 minutes! (Of course the pros need the practice...we don't.) We are foolish enough to think we can jump out of the car...take a few vicious practice swings...and hit the ball far and straight! We are always impressed with the great skills a concert pianist fluidly exhibits...and with the beautiful music we hear. We *must* know that it took countless numbers of daily hours to attain such skills. Most young piano students end up playing "Chopsticks" - for life. Most of us cannot...or will not...devote time to daily practice...so we must settle for a "Chopsticks" ver-

sion of the golf swing...or some point in between. Not too many years ago, a famous touring pro decided to change his grip slightly. He took a week off...hit 700 shots a day for 7 days...to get used to a 1/4" change in hand position! (You and I fully expect to change our entire swing...with one bucket of practice balls.) Don't expect more from golf than you can put into it. Devote as much time as you can to practice. Develop as much skill as you are able to under the circumstances. Settle for some close resemblance to a correct swing...and enjoy the game! Unless you have high ambitions in golf - relax and enjoy the social and aesthetic values in the game. After all, it is more fun to play than practice.

3. Repeated physical movement in an unfamiliar pattern causes muscle soreness...until our bodies become conditioned and accustomed to the new pattern. Seems logical and basic - yet some people do not expect to be sore...even though they do little with their hands and arms in their daily routines. We cannot count the number of times we have had to explain to new golfers that their hands *must* hurt after a solid hour of instruction and/or a practice...holding the club in an unfamiliar way - such as the golf grip. They are not gripping incorrectly - just gripping.

4. We will have good days...and bad days...in all our pursuits. Even on our best days we will hit some bad shots. We cannot possibly hit only good shots - in any round. On a good day we will simply hit a higher percentage of good shots. Tuesday we may have our best skills at our command...play well and be happy. Wednesday - for reasons we will never understand - we may play poorly. This is a human characteristic we must understand. Perhaps if we can accept this phenomenon...we will relax and have a better day than originally supposed.

5. Tension...or doubt...can inhibit even the most highly developed skills. You have been hitting nice shots for five holes...now, here off the sixth tee, some sadist put a lake directly in front of you. You have just hit 12 shots - any one of which would easily go over the lake. But you forget the good shots...stare at the lake...picture the ball going in...convince yourself you are going to hit one in...take out an old ball because you don't want to hit your good one in...now what do you suppose will happen to your shot? The tension will cause you to take a bad swing and chances are great that you *will* hit into the lake. (Pick out that nice area across the lake to land in...think about the many nice shots you have just hit...and swing normally. Who cares what's *under* a nicely-arched shot?) We hit nice shots on the practice range or when we are with our instructor...and don't understand why we cannot do the same on a golf course. The tension and excitement of playing the game...or trying to show someone how well we can do...play tricks with our swings. Most of us react differently under pressure...no matter how slight. (If we put a 10 foot beam on the ground, you would have no problem walking it - perhaps you would even try a few daring stunts. Now let's raise the beam 12 feet into the air...something is different! We would not walk as skillfully or as confidently.) Until you get more playing experience and start feeling more relaxed on a course, it is important that you play with people who are patient and tolerant...people whose company you enjoy. Take the time in every round of golf to enjoy the many positive benefits around you. Enjoy the beauty of the golf course. Notice the pleasant environment you are in. (You could be working or in class you know...how lucky to be on a golf course!)

A POSITIVE ATTITUDE

We can do so much for ourselves...or to ourselves...by the way we think. Those of you who have not discovered the rewards and pleasure in positive thinking are trying to operate on fewer cylinders than are available to you. The influence of attitude is a basic human characteristic.

"If our minds can make us *ill*...which we all have experienced...and accept...doesn't it stand to reason that our minds can make us *well*?" We have always firmly believed this. We teach this in our classes and cannot understand why everyone with a little imagination does not regularly employ this most valuable human ability."

If we stand at the tee and stare at the lake before us...and picture the ball going in...why can't we instead stand there and picture a nice golf swing hitting a beautiful shot onto that nice grassy spot on the fairway over the lake? Your body listens to your head...think about it!

No game in the world lends itself so completely to mental influence as does golf. Things happen fast in other sports and we physically respond because of training and instinct. In golf we have time to ponder every shot. Our thinking has a great influence on the execution of a skillful swing and hit. We can condition ourselves to bring our *best* swings into play in each hit. If we practice and play with a positive attitude...our heads will work *with* us!

MENTAL REHEARSAL

There is scientific evidence now which proves that you can actually rehearse physical movements by replaying them in your mind. If your body has experienced the correct golf swing several times, you can practice that swing by picturing and thinking about beautiful golf swings.

With limited time for actual practice, you can do yourself some good by closing your eyes...*relaxing*...and "seeing and feeling" yourself in nice golf swings.

As you walk down the fairway to your ball...choose the next spot you want your ball in...stare at it...picture several beautiful shots to the spot with the club you intend to use.

A highly successful touring pro was recently asked why he takes so few practice swings when playing. His reply "But I do...before each shot I take several gorgeous swings...up here in my head."

ON THE COURSE - KEEP IT SIMPLE

The practice range is the place to correct swing faults, develop skill, work with more difficult clubs, and to develop confidence in your swing. When you are on the golf course, you are *playing* the game. You must now go along with whatever is working for you. If you are fading the ball and cannot quickly figure out why...aim a little left...and play your fade...and then vow to work on it in your next practice session. On the course you are concerned with playing conditions, distances, club selection, wind factors and positive thinking...you cannot clutter your mind with details of the golf swing.

Keep your thinking simple! Boil the swing fundamentals down to one or two basic clues you have discovered in practice and swing away! Check your grip...alignment (direction)...clubface position...take a smooth backswing...and think only of swinging out *through* the ball...reaching out for your target on each shot.

Use the clubs you have confidence in. There is no rule dictating what clubs *must* be used in play. Use the ones you like...the ones you know will work best for you.

Several years ago, one of the fine college teams averaged 74 strokes per player - per round - for the season. In a fun round after the season, they played using only #5 and #7 irons, and putters...and averaged *76* strokes per player!

The first few rounds you play we would suggest you use only the easier clubs. Use the #3 wood off the tee...a #5 iron down the fairway...and the shorter clubs when close enough to the green.

The learning process takes time...*give* it *time*...keep it simple...let golf grow on you.

ON ADVICE FROM OTHERS

It is traditional in golf to give advice to others - even if unwelcome. It seems to be a part of every social round. Perhaps because of our own frustrations with the intricacy and challenge involved, we feel an instinctive obligation to help others. Beginners are vulnerable...and wives, girlfriends and youngsters are particularly vulnerable.

We have been angered many times over the years watching wives driven to tears...and youngsters driven from golf by ridiculous expectations from perhaps well-meaning - but impatient and intolerant husbands, boyfriends, and fathers. Many times we have observed golf swings being taught with difficult to understand instructions...and continuous streams of suggestions...usually by someone who has spent many years in the game...and expecting the harassed pupil to learn the swing in one hour.

Take lessons from an experienced teacher. Tell your well-meaning friends it is less confusing to listen only to your teacher.

Play your first few rounds on an uncrowded golf course...with patient, tolerant people who understand you are a beginner and will help you with rules, etiquette, and the routine of play.

ON TAKING LESSONS

Do not spend your money on golf instruction unless you intend to practice in between lessons. A teacher can only explain and show you what you need to correct, or work on, in your swing...the development process is left to you. (A doctor can diagnose, prescribe and make suggestions...but the healing process is in *your* hands...or head.) A teacher cannot *give* you skill or make you practice.

Don't take a lesson if you have had a few drinks. The golf swing at best requires rhythm, timing and fine coordination...and the learning process requires receptive thinking and concentration. Take a lesson only if you are fit and ready...or you are wasting your money.

LEFT HAND OR RIGHT?

An idea which happily has been refuted is that left handers should play right-handed because they will have strong left arm control of the swing. (So why don't right handers play left-handed?) Left-handed people should play from their natural side. There is left-handed equipment easily available today.

If a left-handed person has a great deal of athletic ability...then perhaps he/she could start right-handed...only because they will see more good right hand swings to copy...than left.

ABOVE ALL - ENJOY!

Golf is an interesting and extremely challenging game...played in nature's finest settings...with little risk of injury. Golf does not require a high degree of physical fitness or conditioning.

"You can easily forget your problems on a golf course...because you take on a whole *new* set of problems!"

Learn to enjoy the many, many plus factors in the game. Even if you enjoy competition and continually drive yourself to improvement and better scores...take some time in each round...or play an occasional round...for the simple joys and contentment inherent in the game.

"If you have not witnessed and appreciated the majestic serenity of a golf course early in the morning...or late in the evening...you are missing one of nature's gifts to *you*!"

Learn the grand old game of golf...then enjoy golf - the game of a lifetime...any may you enjoy it for many years!!!

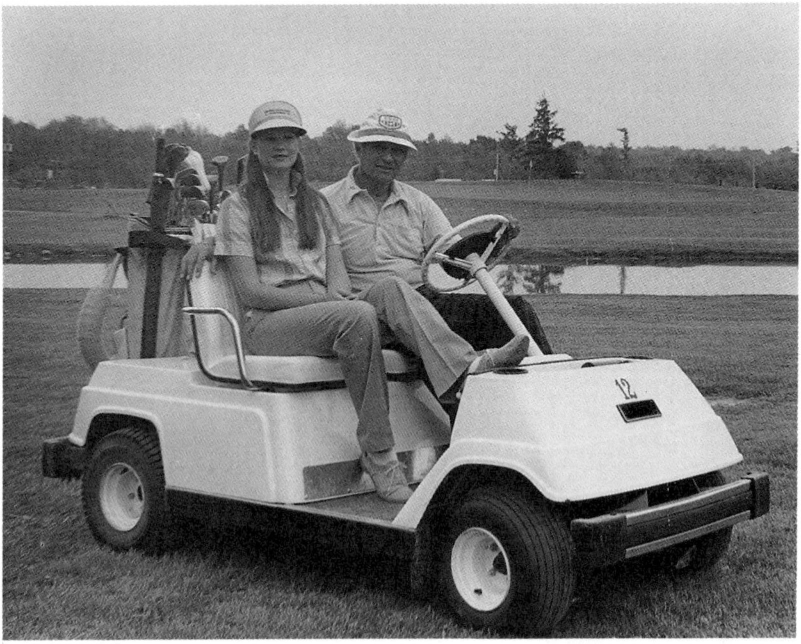
12

Chapter 7

KNOW THE LANGUAGE

Ace	A hole in one...from the tee into the cup.
Address	A player's position just before the swing...includes grip, stance and body position.
Approach Shot	A shot within reach of the green.
Apron	A collar-like area of shortly clipped grass surrounding the green.
Away	The player whose ball is farthest from the hole...and next to hit.
Backspin	A reverse spin on the ball which causes it to slow down...or bounce back when landing. All well-played shots have a degree of backspin on them.
Banana Ball	A slice...a ball which curves from left to right.
Best Ball	An event or game in which two players or four play as a team and the lowest score on a hole is recorded for the team.
Bite	The action of a ball hitting the green with a lot of backspin on it.

Birdie	A score of one stroke under par on any hole.
Blind Bogey	An event in casual play in which a player selects a number...which subtracted from his score in the upcoming round will net a score between 70 and 80. The winning score (between 70 and 80) is drawn out of a hat after the round.
Blind Shot	A shot in which the intended green is not visible.
Bogey	A score of one over par on a hole.
Brassie	A #2 wood...found only in older sets and not included in modern sets.
Break	The slant or slope of the green.
Bunker	A depressed area covered with sand...more commonly called a sand trap. An intentionally placed obstacle and hazard.
Caddie	A person who carries a player's clubs on the course, watches the golf balls, attends the flagsticks and may give advice.
Casual Water	A temporary accumulation of water...not intended as a hazard.
Chip Shot	A short shot from the edge of a green.
Closed Face	The clubface turned to the left rather than square.
Closed Stance	Right foot pulled back from the intended line at the address.
Cup	The plastic or metal lining placed in each hole...4 1/4" in diameter...with a reservoir holder for the flagstick.
Divot	A piece of turf taken out in a shot...which should be replaced and tramped down.
Dog Leg	A fairway which bends to the right or left.

Dormie	When a player or team in a match is leading an opponent by the same number as holes left to play.
Double Bogey	A score of two over par on a hole.
Down	The number of holes or strokes a player or team is behind in a match.
Draw	A shot which curves slightly from right to left.
Drive	A shot from the tee area. The first shot of a hole.
Driver	The #1 wood club.
Drop	When moving the ball according to the rules...in penalty or non-penalty situations...the ball is dropped facing your green with your arm laterally extended to the side.
Dub	A poor shot...usually one which rolls along the ground.
Duffer	A poor, unskilled golfer...also called a "hacker".
Eagle	A score two under par on a hole.
Explosion	A blast shot from a sandtrap.
Fade	A shot which curves slightly from left to right.
Fairway	A mowed area from tee to green...the desired path to the green.
Fat Shot	A shot in which the club hits the turf behind the ball first.
Flagstick	The thin, movable pole...6 - 8' tall to which the flag is attached and designating the hole.
Flat Swing	A swing which is less upright than normal.

Flight	The path of the ball in the air...also the division of players...ranked according to ability...for a tournament.
Follow-Through	The phase of the swing after the ball has been struck.
Fore	A warning cry for anyone in the path of a ball.
Fore Caddie	A person who is sent out to watch balls hit into blind areas.
Foursome	Four players in a group...a standard playing format.
Forward Press	A slight movement forward with the legs or hands prior to the start of the backswing.
Frog's Hair	The apron surrounding a green.
Gimmie	A slang expression for a conceded putt...counts as one more stroke.
Gowf	Probably the original Scotch name for golf...which means "striking with the hand."
Grain	The direction in which the grass on a green is growing. Greens will vary in "grain" on a course.
Green	The putting surface in which the hole is cut and flag placed. The most closely-cropped grass on a course.
Grip	The handle of a club...and the player's grasp of a club.
Gross Score	A player's actual score on a hole or for a round...with no handicap strokes deducted.
Ground Under Repair	A stake or lined area in which work is being done. A ball in this area may be lifted and dropped.
Halve	To tie a hole.

Know the Language 103

Handicap	A number figure which ranks players as to degree of ability. Also a figure on the scorecard which ranks a hole in degree of difficulty in comparison to the other holes on that course. (And an old joke: Tom - "What is my handicap?" Dave - "Probably your golf swing.")
Hazard	A bunker (sandtrap), creek, lake or ditch...which is played according to special USGA rules.
Head	The hitting part of a club at the lower end of the shaft.
Heel	The part of the clubface where the shaft enters the head.
High Side	The area above and beyond the hole on a sloping green.
Hole High	A ball even with the hole...off to one side.
Hole Out	To finish a hole by stroking the ball into the cup.
Honor	The privilege of hitting first on a tee...granted to the lowest scorer on the previous hole.
Hood	Closing the clubface and decreasing the loft.
Hook	A shot which curves from right to left.
Hosel	The part of a clubhead into which the shaft fits. Also called the "neck".
In	The second nine holes in an eighteen hole round.
Inside-Out	The path of the clubhead in a correct swing which moves from left to right during impact.
Interlock	A type of grip in which the left forefinger and right little finger are intertwined.

Irons	The clubs in a set whose heads are metal...not including the putter.
LPGA	Ladies Professional Golf Association.
Lag	The first putt when a long distance from the cup.
Lateral Water Hazard	A water hazard which runs parallel or in the same direction as the fairway.
Lie	The position of the ball. Also refers to the angle formed by the shaft and sole of a club.
Links	Another name for a golf course.
Lip	The edge of a hole.
Loft	The backward angle of a clubface. Also the trajectory of a shot.
Loose Impediment	A natural object (not growing) such as leaves, grass, rocks, pebbles, twigs...which may be removed...*without* moving the ball, except in a hazard.
Low Side	The area below the hole on a sloping green.

Marker
1. Wood, iron or plastic objects used on tees to designate specific hitting areas. On any tee you will find red (ladies'), white (mens') and blue (championship) markers.
2. White out of bounds stakes and red hazard stakes.
3. Small coin or plastic object used to mark and remove a ball from the putting surface.
4. A person who is assigned to keep score for a group in a tournament is also called a "marker".

Mashie	An old term for a #5 iron.
Match Play	A competitive event based on the number of holes won or lost, rather than on strokes.

Medal Play	A competitive game based on number of strokes used.
Medalist	The person scoring the lowest gross score in a tournament round.
Mid-Iron	An old term for a #2 iron.
Mulligan	In social golf...a second shot from the tee if the first one is a poor one. Each player is allowed one "mulligan".
Nassau	A friendly wager event...in which three points are awarded...and bet on: one for each nine...and one for the eighteen holes.
Neck	The part of a club where the shaft enters the head. Also called the "hosel."
Net	The score for a hole or a round after the player's handicap has been deducted.
Niblick	An old term for the current #9 iron. (In the old days there was no #9 iron...this term applied to the #8 then.)
Obstruction	Refers to artificial, man-made objects such as: benches, shelters, water fountains, ball washers, etc.
Open Face	A clubface which is pointed to the right of the intended line at the address.
Open Stance	Left foot pulled back slightly from the parallel...or intended line of flight.
Out of Bounds	Areas marked with white stakes beyond which play is not permitted. A penalty situation.
Out	The first nine on an eighteen hole course.
Outside-In	A swing, from right to left, across the ball and across the intended line of flight. The most common swing error in golf.

Overclubbing	Using a longer club than needed for the distance desired.
Overlap	The most popular form of grip...in which the right little finger overlaps the left forefinger.
Par	A standard of excellence as a score on a hole...based on the length of the hole.
Penalty Stroke	A stroke added to your score for various rule infractions and movement from trouble areas.
PGA	The Men's Professional Golf Association
Pin	Another name for the flagstick.
Pin High	Same as "hole high."
Playing Through	Passing through the group ahead. They should allow you through if they are slower and there is room for your group ahead of them...or if they will take time to look for a lost ball.
Preferred Lies	Rules used in adverse conditions which allow a movement and cleaning of the ball.
Press	Playing too hard...and also a version of doubling the bet in a friendly wager game.
Pull	A shot which is hit straight, but is far off target to the left.
Punch	A low, firmly-hit shot used into the wind or under tree branches.
Push	A shot which is hit straight, but far off target to the right.
Putter	The club used on the green to roll the ball into the cup...also the person putting.
Rough	The deeper or heavier grass out-side the fairways.

"Rub of the Green"	An unpredictable, tough luck happening to a ball..."*that's the way the ball bounces.*"
Sand Trap	A bunker filled with sand...a hazard.
Scotch Foursome	A two-person team event...in which one ball is used...hit alternately, after the better tee shot is selected.
Scratch Player	A fine player who is rated with-out a handicap.
Setup	The address position.
Shaft	The long, stick-like portion of a club to which the grip and head are attached.
Shank	A miss-hit which causes the ball to go sharply to the right.
Sky	A high, pop-up shot...one which "might bring rain."
Slice	A spinning shot which curves the ball from left to right. The most common miss-hit among male golfers.
Slope	A method which rates the difficulty of a golf course so as to make individual handicaps more flexible and fair when playing a variety of courses. The SLOPE of a course is determined by a professional group for a fee.
Snake	To knock in a long putt.
Sole	The bottom surface of a club...rests on the ground at the address.
Spoon	An old term for the #3 wood.
Square Stance	Toes placed at the address in a line parallel to the intended line of flight.
Stance	The position of the feet in the address position.

Stiff	To hit the ball close to the pin.
Stroke Play	Same as medal play.
Stymie	Anther ball closely in front of yours obstructing your shot. Also an obsolete putting situation.
Sudden Death	If a match is tied after the round, extra holes are played to determine the winner.
Summer Rules	The ball must be played as it lies everywhere...and moved only under USGA rules.
Sweet Spot	Hitting the ball in the absolute center of the clubhead..."hitting it on the screws."
Take-away	The initial move in the backswing.
Target	Your objective for each shot.
Tee	The wooden or plastic peg put into the ground on which to place the ball for the *first* shot of a hole only. Also refers to the whole tee-off area for each hole.
Tee Markers	Red, white, blue or gold sets of markers designating specific hitting areas on each tee.
Texas Wedge	Using a putter off the green...or rolling the ball out of a trap which has a shallow bank.
Through the Green	The area of a golf hole from the tee to the cup.
Threesome	Three players playing as a group.
Tight lie	A ball down in the grass close to the earth surface.
Toe	The front tip of the clubhead.

Know the Language

Top	To hit the top-half of the ball causing it to roll or bounce along the ground without loft. A common female miss-hit.
Underclub	Using a shorter club than needed for the distance desired.
Unplayable Lie	A ball declared unplayable by a player...who chooses to take a stroke penalty for moving it.
Up	The number of holes or strokes a player is ahead of his opponent.
Upright Swing	A swing which is too erect or too vertical.
USGA	The United States Golf Association; the ruling body in American golf.
Waggle	The back and forth preliminary motion at the time of address and before the swing.
Water Hole	A hole which has a water hazard somewhere between the tee and green.
Wedge	A special, high-lofted club designed for high approach shots. A #10 iron. A sand wedge is a heavy-flanged club designed for sand-trap shots and heavy grass.
Whiff	To swing at the ball and miss it completely...counts as a stroke.
Winter Rules	Rules which allow the player to improve lies...generally in the fairway only.
Woods	The clubs with wooden heads.

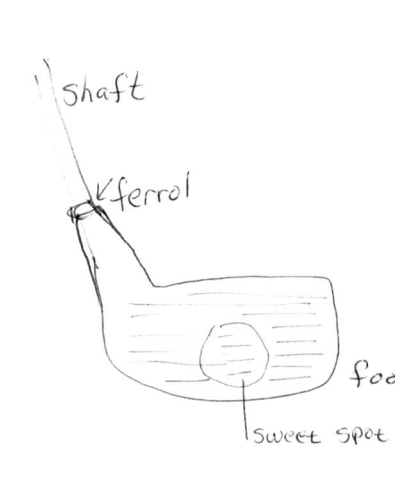

need tees -
glove -
balls -

NOTES

shaft
ferrol
foot
sweet spot

etiquette - replace divots
never take your clubs upon the tee
watch for others ball

penalties - hit someone else's golf ball

Note 2 for Test

<u>Free drop</u> -
① <u>casual water</u> (water squishing at stance)
never take it closer to the hole
② ground under repair
③ Burrowing animal hole
④ <u>man made objects</u> (one club length) or one more
cart path - nearest point of relief (edge)

Note Two for Test

NOTES

1 stroke penalties — what ever is part of the Golf course.

① Unplayable Lie
   (you can move 2 club lengths)
② Water hazard
   take your ball & move it back around the lake.
③ Lost Ball (5 minutes look)
   go back to the tee & hit another one
   or back to your last hit zone.
④ Out of Bounds — out of the white stakes
   hitting a provisional Ball & playing when you have declared your 1st play out of bounds.
⑤ ~~Forgetting to~~ ~~Asking~~ for permission to identify Ball
⑥ Moving debris from behind the Ball

Note two for test

2 stroke Penalty

① hitting the wrong ball
② Flag stik hitting (remove it) when you are on the green
③ hitting another persons ball up on tee.
④ unsportman like conduct

NOTES